D1309128

Compelled by Love

A Journey to Missional Living

PHILIP NATION
WITH ED STETZER

LifeWay Press®
Nashville, Tennessee

Published by LifeWay Press®

© 2008 Ed Stetzer and Philip Nation

Third printing 2010

ISBN 978-1-4158-7123-2

Item 005426308

Dewey decimal classification: 266

Subject headings: MISSIONS \ EVANGELISTIC WORK

Unless otherwise noted, all Scripture quotations are taken from the Holman Christian Standard Bible®, Copyright © 1999, 2000, 2002, 2003, 2009 by Holman Bible Publishers. Used by permission. Holman Christian Standard Bible®, Holman CSB®, and HCSB® are federally registered trademarks of Holman Bible Publishers. Scripture quotations marked NIV are taken from the Holy Bible, New International Version, copyright © 1973, 1978, 1984 by International Bible Society.

To order additional copies of this resource, write to LifeWay Church Resources Customer Service; One LifeWay Plaza; Nashville, TN 37234-0113; fax (615) 251-5933; e-mail *orderentry@lifeway.com*; phone toll free (800) 458-2772; order online at *www.lifeway.com*; or visit the LifeWay Christian Store serving you.

Printed in the United States of America

Leadership and Adult Publishing

LifeWay Church Resources

One LifeWay Plaza

Nashville, TN 37234-0175

Contents

WEEK 1: MISSIONAL LIVING
Small-Group Experience 8
Devotions. 14

WEEK 2: OUR MISSIONARY GOD
Small-Group Experience 32
Devotions. 38

WEEK 3: OUR MISSIONAL ENDEAVOR
Small-Group Experience 56
Devotions. 62

WEEK 4: MAKING A MISSIONAL IMPACT
Small-Group Experience 80
Devotions. 86

WEEK 5: MISSIONAL SPIRITUALITY
Small-Group Experience 104
Devotions. 110

WEEK 6: MISSIONAL OBEDIENCE
Small-Group Experience 130
Devotions. 136

WEEK 7: LAUNCHING INTO MISSION
Small-Group Experience 154

My Mission List 158

Christian Growth Study Plan 159

The Authors

PHILIP NATION is the director of ministry development at LifeWay Christian Resources. Having followed God's call into the ministry at age 16, he has worked in a number of areas of ministry, including youth minister, single-adult minister, senior pastor, and education minister at a seven-thousand-member church. Prior to coming to LifeWay, Philip served as a church planter with the North American Mission Board, where he and Ed Stetzer served on a team to plant a new church in north Georgia.

Philip coauthored *Compelled by Love: The Most Excellent Way to Missional Living* and contributed to Ed Stetzer's *Breaking the Missional Code*, *Comeback Churches*, and *Planting Missional Churches*. He has also authored numerous articles in print and on the Web.

Philip holds a BA in religion from Samford University and an MDiv from Beeson Divinity School. He is completing a doctor of ministry at the Southern Baptist Theological Seminary. He and his wife, Angie, have two sons, Andrew and Chris.

ED STETZER is the president of LifeWay Research and missiologist in residence at LifeWay Christian Resources. Ed has planted churches in New York, Pennsylvania, and Georgia and has trained church planters and pastors across the United States and on five continents.

Ed holds a BS from Shorter College, an MDiv from the Southern Baptist Theological Seminary, an MA in religion from Liberty Baptist Theological Seminary, a DMin from Beeson Divinity School, and a PhD from the Southern Baptist Theological Seminary.

Ed is the author of *Planting New Churches in a Postmodern Age*, *Perimeters of Light: Biblical Boundaries for the Emerging Church* (with Elmer Towns), *Breaking the Missional Code* (with David Putman), *Planting Missional Churches*, *Comeback Churches* (with Mike Dodson), *11 Innovations in the Local Church* (with Elmer Towns and Warren Bird), and *Compelled by Love: The Most Excellent Way to Missional Living* (with Philip Nation).

INTRODUCTION

Welcome to the study of *Compelled by Love*. During the weeks to come, you will go on a journey to deepen your understanding of God's character and mission. Though there are many biblical descriptions of God, one stands out with simple but profound clarity: "God is love" (1 John 4:8). God wants to share His great love with all people who will accept the salvation He offers through His Son, Jesus Christ. In this study you will learn that God also wants you, as His ambassador, to reflect His character and to join His redemptive mission. By gaining a missional perspective on life, you can make a difference in your church and community for the glory of God.

God's love has both eternal and everyday implications for our lives. As Christians, we are called to participate in His mission to expand the kingdom of God. The *what* of ministry is to declare God's greatness and to call people to respond to the gospel. But sometimes the *why* of ministry escapes us. We should do the right thing, but we simply don't have the motivation.

The early church also needed to be taught the *why* behind the *what* of ministry. In his second letter to the Corinthian church, the apostle Paul taught, "Christ's love compels us, since we have reached this conclusion: if One died for all, then all died. And He died for all so that those who live should no longer live for themselves, but for the One who died for them and was raised" (2 Cor. 5:14-15).

Love for Christ was Paul's central compulsion for his life and ministry, affecting his thoughts, motivation, and activity. Though Paul's life was completely centered on the glory of God through the work of the gospel, he was motivated by the principle of love in all he did.

This seven-session study will help you evaluate the state of your heart. As you live your daily life, love for God and for people should guide your thoughts, motivation, and activity. Living a biblical love, which is sacrificial in nature, will help you look beyond your wants and preferences to the issues of God's kingdom and others' needs.

Each week you will engage in both group and personal activities. We suggest that you follow this outline to benefit from the study personally and as a group:

- Greet one another, pray, and discuss the previous week's devotions (10 min.).
- Watch a DVD segment (10 to 15 min.).
- Discuss the DVD segment and questions provided in the group experience (35 min.).
- Close with prayer.

For sessions 1–6, you will find five personal devotions that follow each session. Designed to reinforce the previous group experience, the devotions will help you deepen your understanding of missional living and apply missional concepts to your life. In the seventh and final session, you will discuss the lessons learned and the changes group members are making in their lives to be compelled by love.

Each week we hope you will rediscover and deepen your love for God as you respond to the great love He has for you and for all the world. We pray that you and your group members will find a renewed sense of passion for God's glory as you study *Compelled by Love* together.

SESSION

1

Missional Living

SESSION GOAL

You will identify the right motivation
for missional living and honestly
evaluate your perspective
on life and mission.

Motivation for Being on Mission

→ **What is your normal perspective on your work?**

- Just get it done.
- Do it right the first time.
- All of this has major consequences.
- I wish I could do something different.
- Why won't anyone help me?
- I'm glad to serve.

→ **What motivates you? What is the driving force in your life? If you had to choose the one thing that motivated you most (and be honest!), what would you say it is? Why?**

Watch DVD session 1.

What is missional living?

Read 2 Corinthians 5:14-21:

Christ's love compels us, since we have reached this conclusion: If One died for all, then all died. And He died for all so that those who live should no longer live for themselves, but for the One who died for them and was raised. From now on, then, we do not know anyone in a purely human way. Even if we have known Christ in a purely human way, yet now we no longer know Him in this way. Therefore, if anyone is in Christ, he is a new creation; old things have passed away, and look, new things have come. Everything is from God, who reconciled us to Himself through Christ and gave us the ministry of reconciliation: That is, in Christ, God was reconciling the world to Himself, not counting their trespasses against them, and He has committed the message of reconciliation to us. Therefore, we are ambassadors for Christ, certain that God is appealing through us. We plead on Christ's behalf, "Be reconciled to God." He made the One who did not know sin to be sin for us, so that we might become the righteousness of God in Him.

Paul said, "Christ's love compels us" (v. 14).

⟶ If love became the central compulsion in your life, how would the following areas of your life change?

• Marriage?

• Parenting?

• Work relationships?

• Life with your church family?

• Your study group?

⟶ What conclusion did Paul reach that compelled him to live with love as the guiding force in his life (see vv. 14-15)?

⟶ How does living for the One who died for us—the living Lord Jesus—affect the way we love others?

What Is the Gospel?

In the DVD segment Ed Stetzer gave a working definition of *gospel*.

→ **If you had only 60 seconds to tell someone the basic parts of the gospel, what would you say? In other words, what are the essential truths of the gospel?**

→ **How does accepting Christ change our eternal destiny?**

Christ's Perspective on People

Paul warns us not to view people in a "purely human way" (v. 16) any longer. In contrast, we often define one another and ourselves by what we do and whom we know.

→ **List specific ways you define yourself and other people.**

→ **How does viewing people in a "purely human way" affect our interest in their eternal destiny?**

According to 2 Corinthians 5:14-21, Christ's work changes our perspective about people.

→ Name ways Christ's love is different from the image of love we see portrayed in movies and on TV.

→ How could you change the way you perceive your neighbors to reflect the way Christ views them? What could you do to show them you have a changed perspective on them?

Not only are we to view people in our community from a new perspective, but we are also to see ourselves in a new way as well.

→ List ways salvation changes the way we live.

Being on Mission

→ When you know a missionary is going to speak at church, what is your reaction?

- Enthusiastically attend the service
- Hope the pastor will still preach a sermon
- Just wish it could be over
- Skip the service altogether

Your reaction to hearing a missionary speak has much to do with your view of missionary work.

→ **Which of the following qualify as mission work? Check all that apply.**

- Doing projects and sharing the gospel in other countries
- Taking a short trip to another location for construction or evangelistic work
- Dedicating your entire life to live far away from home
- Working for a career missionary
- Sharing Christ in your everyday routine

Ambassadors for Christ

We are to represent the King because God has called us to be "ambassadors for Christ" (v. 20).

→ **What is the primary work of an ambassador?**

→ **What would be the results if we were poor ambassadors?**

→ **What appeal should we make to lost people in our communities (see v. 20)?**

Conclusion

→ **What connections do you see between love and missional living?**

→ **Close with prayer. Before the next group experience, read the daily devotions for week 1.**

WEEK 1

Missional Living

WHAT IS THE GOSPEL?

To understand missional living, we've got to start with the gospel. The apostle Paul wrote, "Brothers, I want to clarify for you the gospel I proclaimed to you; you received it and have taken your stand on it. You are also saved by it, if you hold to the message I proclaimed to you—unless you believed for no purpose" (1 Cor. 15:1-2). This bold statement left the Corinthian church no choice but to listen intently and to learn the gospel completely. The same must be true for us in our day.

At a church-planting conference where Ed Stetzer spoke, he asked the audience of about 550 church planters to pair up and answer three questions. First, he asked, "What is your new church doing to be culturally relevant?" Immediately, everyone turned to a partner and began to share. After 30 seconds the other person answered the question. A distinct roar of enthusiasm filled the room.

Second, Ed asked the participants, "What is your church doing to engage your community?" Once again, they immediately turned to one another and passionately talked about engaging their communities. The roar gained momentum as each took a turn.

Then Ed asked the third question: "What is the gospel?" An eerie silence fell on the room. If ever there was a moment when missional church leaders would and should answer with a roar, it should have been at this moment. Admittedly, they were caught off guard. But to be honest, both Ed and I were stunned.

Being culturally relevant and engaging the community are essential to doing ministry well. But defining the gospel is the core of ministry. Without it, our churches and individual lives have nothing to offer our neighbors. When we assume the gospel, we assume too much.

Define the gospel in your own words.

Summed up in one word, the gospel is Jesus. Jesus Christ is who He claimed to be. His crucifixion and resurrection are the most important events in human history. The gospel is this: our incarnated God died for our sins so that we could be reconciled to Him and glorify Him eternally. †

DAY 1

Ambassadors of Love

Christ's love compels us, since we have reached this conclusion: If One died for all, then all died. And He died for all so that those who live should no longer live for themselves, but for the One who died for them and was raised. From now on, then, we do not know anyone in a purely human way. Even if we have known Christ in a purely human way, yet now we no longer know Him in this way. Therefore, if anyone is in Christ, he is a new creation; old things have passed away, and look, new things have come. Everything is from God, who reconciled us to Himself through Christ and gave us the ministry of reconciliation: That is, in Christ, God was reconciling the world to Himself, not counting their trespasses against them, and He has committed the message of reconciliation to us. Therefore, we are ambassadors for Christ, certain that God is appealing through us. We plead on Christ's behalf, "Be reconciled to God." He made the One who did not know sin to be sin for us, so that we might become the righteousness of God in Him.

2 CORINTHIANS 5:14-21

In our primary text for this study, Paul wrote to an immature church about the key issue of our lives—redemption. But every believer must understand that the redemption we enjoy also puts us on a path to participate in God's purposes. Verse 20 defines the way we do that: by being "ambassadors for Christ."

What is the primary work of an ambassador?

The office of ambassador has always fascinated me. It seems to be a job with a lot of responsibility but no real authority. The person or government the ambassador represents holds the ultimate authority. As an ambassador, if you do your work well, you are hardly remembered. But if you do it very poorly, you will make the national newscast for sure!

Think of the honor bestowed on an ambassador. Princes and princesses, royal by birth, hold authority simply due to family ties. But an ambassador has no royal blood or pedigree. Rather, a king looks kindly on a common citizen and brings him into a place of power. The ambassador is given a unique task—speaking for the king. When visiting another country, an ambassador is never asked to give his personal opinions. Rather, he is expected to repeat the king's opinion, positions, and directives. It is a great privilege.

Being an ambassador is also a grave responsibility. An ambassador carries the reputation of the king. Whether he is in the realm of an ally or an enemy, he becomes the physical, moral, and verbal representative of the king.

The same privilege and responsibility belong to ambassadors of God.

Review the Scripture passage on page 17. In what ways are Christians ambassadors for Christ?

As ambassadors for Christ, what appeal do we make to lost persons?

Verse 20 teaches that God is making his appeal "through us." Such a statement by the living God is stunning. As the King of kings, He has the power to visit every corner of creation and personally declare His glory. But because of His love for His people, He allows us to declare His offer of redemption.

What an awesome responsibility! Is it any wonder that our Lord requires us to be so careful with our lives and doctrine (see 1 Tim. 4:16)?

God's love is also revealed in His patience. If He personally visited the nations in His power and glory, all would crumble under the weight of His justice. But in His longsuffering love He sends you and me into the world to deliver the imperative "Be reconciled to God" (v. 20).

Evaluate your job performance as an ambassador for Christ. Check the statement that best describes your assessment.

I have never thought of myself as Christ's ambassador.

I would like to live as Christ's ambassador to the lost.

I am faithfully fulfilling the role by sharing the gospel in my daily life.

Paul wrote that Jesus became sin so that we could become righteousness. Though there are myriad ways to describe ambassadorship from a geopolitical perspective, ultimately, the comparisons fail. Earthly ambassadors deal with mundane matters like trillions of dollars in national treasuries, borders of countries, and the rights of citizens. As missionary ambassadors of heaven, we handle the message that God's Son took the judgment for sin and offers the freedom of righteousness for humankind! These matters now reside in your hands, your mind, and your soul. †

On page 158 make a list of persons you know who are not believers to whom you can be an ambassador of God's love. Start praying for opportunities to share the good news of Christ with them.

Refer to your mission list throughout the study so that you can regularly add to it and pray for your friends by name.

DAY 2
Motivated by Love

Dear friends, let us love one another, because love is from God, and everyone who loves has been born of God and knows God. The one who does not love does not know God, because God is love. God's love was revealed among us in this way: God sent His One and Only Son into the world so that we might live through Him. Love consists in this: not that we loved God, but that He loved us and sent His Son to be the propitiation for our sins. Dear friends, if God loved us in this way, we also must love one another. No one has ever seen God. If we love one another, God remains in us and His love is perfected in us.

1 JOHN 4:7-12

On most days we know *what* we should do. Whether from Bible study lessons, sermons, or personal devotions in the Word, we have learned what to do. And look at you—you just began a study about missional living! Most of us do not struggle with what we should do. We struggle with the motivation to do it.

The apostle John often wrote of love in his Gospel account and the three letters he wrote under God's inspiration.

Review the passage above. How did God show His love for us?

Because God loved us, what does He expect us to do in response?

What is the connection between love and missional living?

This passage confronts us with the fact that God's love is connected to the way we live. Love is more than *what* we should do; it is the *why* of all missional living.

The Bible clearly teaches that when you have love, you follow it with action. Love shows itself: "God's love was revealed among us in this way: God sent His One and Only Son" (v. 9). Love serves as the source of the action and not the other way around. Don't be deceived by a "Fake it till you make it" mentality that desires to do the right things but never connects to the heart of God. The end is predictable: you will fail because you don't have the connection to the source of love, God Himself.

What is the primary motivation that keeps you going when dealing with difficult people?

▨ **Strong work ethic**	▨ **Love**
▨ **Perseverance**	▨ **Patience**

Love can be a buoy for ministry. Even when navigating the rough waters of people's problems and sinfulness, love can keep us afloat. When we lose patience, are tempted by frustration, or simply feel tired, Christ's love within us is the only never-ceasing motivation for missional living.

There is no doubt that living as a missionary is difficult, whether at home or abroad. My friends Wes and Tamara serve as missionaries in Romania. In America they had comfortable lives, serving as lay leaders in a great church. But now they live and work in a poor neighborhood without the comforts they enjoyed here. Why did they make such a change? They fully loved God, and He developed in them a fearless love for the Romanian people.

Where does our love stand toward God? It should be one of full devotion. If it is not, we must choose to move toward it and trust in His ability to mature it within us. As it grows, our King can mature our love for the people He has assigned to us. For me, it could be the rowdy teenagers in my neighborhood. For you, His assignment may be the white-collar working moms who come home tired each evening or the blue-collar men who cannot seem to get ahead in life. Each of their lives comes with emotional baggage, painful experiences, and real sin. In other words, it's messy. Only by loving them as God loved us will we dare to extend our efforts and lives to touch them with the message of Christ's redemption. †

Think about the lost persons you listed yesterday on your mission list (p. 158). Do you love them the way Christ loves you?

Reread 1 John 4:7-16 and grasp the full force of verse 8. If you do not love others, you do not know God. Do you know for certain that you know God and seek to live in His love?

Go to the Lord and ask Him to give you a heart to reach out to others with His love.

DAY 3
The Greatest Commandment

One of the scribes approached. When he heard them debating and saw that Jesus answered them well, he asked Him, "Which command is the most important of all?"

"This is the most important," Jesus answered: "Listen, Israel! The Lord our God, the Lord is One. Love the Lord your God with all your heart, with all your soul, with all your mind, and with all your strength. The second is: Love your neighbor as yourself. There is no other command greater than these."

MARK 12:28-31

We are on mission because we want to follow Christ in obedience. So when He identifies the Greatest Commandment, it's time to listen and learn. Mark's record of this moment in Jesus' life is different from the other Gospels because of one significant factor: Jesus began his statement by quoting Deuteronomy 6:4-5, which includes the Shema. The Shema is generally considered the most ancient theological decree of the Hebrew people. Facing a world obsessed with a multitude of gods and goddesses, the people of God stood firm, proclaiming that there is only one God; and He is, as Israel declared, "the LORD our God" (Deut. 6:4).

Perhaps the reason love becomes lost in the ocean of humanity is that we have begun our conversations about love without a declaration of humility before God. Consider your own life.

Identify the typical state of your heart in each situation. Check one choice for each question.

When your love fades and jealousy replaces it, is the root cause—
▢ your need for things?
▢ your lack of understanding of God's great provision?

When your love retreats and frustration takes root, is it because—
▢ the other person is a jerk?
▢ you have lost touch with God's patience for your own repentance?

When you yank love away from a betraying friend, is it due to—
▢ a damaged ego?
▢ the loss of perspective that God has a desire for their redemption?

Once we acknowledge the truth that God is without equal and has no rivals, we can only conclude that we must love Him supremely. His character must be motivation enough for us to give up all else in order to love Him utterly.

In the narrative of Mark 12, Jesus, when questioned by someone who should have known the answer, lays forth an answer with zero wiggle room. Our love for God should spring from every arena of life—heart, soul, mind, and strength. We must adore Him without reservation.

Our first duty as Christians is to know and love God. With that as the surest foundation, only then can we move on to other matters of His kingdom.

Why is supremely loving God foundational to missional living?

When we confess our faith in God and choose to love Him, being missional begins to gain momentum in our lives. As we press our lives toward God, we can allow Him to press our lives outward on the mission He has set out for us.

As you pray about the place of Christ in your heart, consider Jesus' words in Matthew 10:37-38: "The person who loves father or mother more than Me is not worthy of Me; the person who loves son or daughter more than Me is not worthy of Me. And whoever doesn't take up his cross and follow Me is not worthy of Me." Your love for Him must be greater than for any other. It can be, and it will be as you recognize God's greatness and wish all to know Him as the Lord of their lives. †

The Great Commandment identifies four arenas of life that should be consumed by our love for Christ. Beside each one, list a way you could love God more completely.

Heart (emotions):

Soul (spiritual life):

Mind (thought life):

Strength (physical activity):

DAY 4
The Almost Greatest Commandment

"This is the most important," Jesus answered: "Listen, Israel! The Lord our God, the Lord is One. Love the Lord your God with all your heart, with all your soul, with all your mind, and with all your strength. The second is: Love your neighbor as yourself. There is no other command greater than these."

MARK 12:29-31

Admit it. You've looked out a window of your home and thought, *My neighbors surely are weird.* Unfortunately, I must tell you some disturbing news about them: they've looked at you and said the same thing.

How well do you know your neighbors? List those closest to your house, along with any eccentricities you have noticed.

Living in a subdivision is not the only thing Christ had in mind when He commanded us to love our neighbors, but it is one of the things. And for those of us living in modern America, loving our weird neighbors is a great test case for the principle behind Christ's commands.

But don't overlook the last sentence of verse 31: "There is no other command greater than these." Intellectually and spiritually, I understand God's requirement for me to love Him above all other people and things.

I'm not always obedient, but I get it. You probably do as well. But loving my neighbor is sometimes a different matter.

At face value, it just doesn't seem plausible that loving our neighbor is so critical. Yet Christ inseparably placed together the two ideas of loving God and loving others. The spiritual reality to which we are called is to care so much for others that our own lives blissfully fade into the background of life. It is that important!

Think again about the people who live on your street. If you don't know them, make it your mission this month to learn their names, the ages of their children, where they work, and the spiritual condition of the family. Your endgame should be to discover how you can love these people better.

Be forewarned: they will be shocked, surprised, or even scared by a loving neighbor. We have grown accustomed to sniffing out people's underlying motives. So make your motive pure—simply to love your neighbors as Christ would love them if He were present in the flesh.

From the passage we call the parable of the Good Samaritan, Jesus taught that our neighbor is not just someone who lives on our street but whoever is near us, especially someone in need (see Luke 10:30-37).

Identify some of the other neighbors in your life who need Christ's love—a coworker, the grocery clerk, a homeless mom, or your company's wealthy executives. What could you say or do to show that you care about them?

What needs do they have to which you can minister?

Tragedy has struck most of the communities where we live: Christians and churches generally have a bad reputation. Regarded as hypocrites and just generally annoying, we have damaged the reputation of Christ by our unloving behavior. If we are thought of poorly by the world, let it be for the scandal of the cross, not for the scoundrels among us. Knowing the temptations we face as believers, God has already given the prescription: "By this all people will know that you are my disciples, if you have love for one another" (John 13:35). We have a message that separates our speech and behavior from the rest of humanity. Accompanying the message of the cross should be love for our neighbors. It will seem otherworldly to them— because it is.

As you seek ways to serve your neighbors, you will win an opportunity to present the gospel message to the lost, call home wayward Christians, and encourage members of the body of Christ. †

Choose a neighbor in your life who needs to be served in some way. It might be a person or a family who lives on your street or some-one you interact with on a regular basis. Pray for them and write down several needs you can meet this week to show them the love of Christ. What can you do to show them that you love them?

DAY 5
Fulfilling the Law of Christ

Brothers, if someone is caught in any wrongdoing, you who are spiritual should restore such a person with a gentle spirit, watching out for yourselves so you also won't be tempted. Carry one another's burdens; in this way you will fulfill the law of Christ. For if anyone considers himself to be something when he is nothing, he deceives himself. But each person should examine his own work, and then he will have a reason for boasting in himself alone, and not in respect to someone else. For each person will have to carry his own load.

GALATIANS 6:1-5

Serving as a missional follower of Christ will affect more than just our relationship with God. As we discovered yesterday, loving our neighbor is a portion of Christ's summation of the law. As the apostle Paul wrote to the early Galatian church, there is another law to fulfill—the law of Christ. This passage teaches missional believers how to fulfill the law of Christ.

A *life of restoration*. We will fall. Sometimes we will fall often. Believers are surrounded by the same temptations as everyone else. Yet we have an advantage: we are blessed with the indwelling Spirit of God to empower us so that we can avoid the enticements of the flesh. God will give us strength to endure each temptation. But there will be moments in life when we sin.

As our lives are conformed to that of Christ, we will begin to emulate His own mission—redemption. It is counterintuitive to the way we lived prior to our salvation. The natural human impulse is to use someone else's fall as an opportunity to race ahead of them. Missional living calls us to perceive people's falls differently. A fall carries a significant consequence for the outworking of God's mission in the person's life; therefore, we should intervene on their behalf as God has intervened on ours.

Paul did not tell us to send just anyone to do the work of restoration. He specifically called for those who are "spiritual" (v. 1) to restore the fallen with gentleness. That qualifier of how restoration should occur determines who should engage in the activity.

How does Paul's teaching correspond to your past experiences when people have fallen?

What is the typical response of the church to those who have sinned?
  Restore them.
  Ignore the sin.
  Refuse to associate with them.
  Take them before the church body.

Why do you think God instructs believers to respond redemptively?

A life of compassion. Anyone can bludgeon a sinner with truth and guilt. But a person filled to the brim with the Holy Spirit will gently guide a fallen sibling in God's family back to our Master's service (see v. 1). As we mature in our spiritual lives, our character will reflect that of Christ, which is marked by love.

According to the passage on page 29, how do we fulfill the law of Christ?

How do missional Christians carry one another's burdens?

In fulfilling Christ's law, we must move past mere appearance and invest ourselves personally. Mere appearance can involve ranting, raving, and influencing good behavior through guilt. Christ did not choose these tactics, and neither should we. Paul taught the Galatians to restore while holding a meek disposition. The meekness called for does not equate with powerlessness. Instead, meekness means holding our power in check. As we see fellow believers falter, we should rush to their side with the mind and attitude of Christ toward the weak and fallen.

A life of humility. As you help restore another believer, temptation will visit your door as well.

According to the passage on page 29, what is the great deception believers must guard against?

How do missional Christians avoid this deception?

Knowing our penchant for thinking too much of ourselves, Paul warned us of the self-deception of pride, which might lead us to think, *Look what I have done on behalf of this poor, pitiful, weak believer! I have restored him to wholeness.* Instead of taking that attitude, we must rigorously test ourselves to make sure we acknowledge the only true source of restoration. Missional living is messy because we are interacting with those who are mired in sin. We as Christians must take every precaution to hide ourselves within our relationship with Christ. Only He can redeem. We are merely clay pots carrying the precious message of redemption (see 2 Cor 4:7). †

What must you do to guard your own spiritual maturity when restoring those who have fallen?

Think about times when fellow believers have fallen into sin and what the church did in response. How could the church have handled these situations in a more redemptive way?

SESSION

2

Our Missionary God

SESSION GOAL

You will explore God's character and recognize that His mission originated in His heart. You will understand that missional ministry can be accomplished only if it is based on the foundation of God's character.

Missional Checkup

→ Describe a time this week when you served as an ambassador for God's kingdom. How did you drop your kingdom and take up God's?

→ Explain how your understanding of God's love changed this week.

→ How did you serve a neighbor this week?

The Father Is Willing to Search

→ Describe your fondest memory of your parents or those who raised you. Explain why this story stands out among the many experiences you had growing up.

→ Describe a time when you were lost and your parents had to look for you.

One obvious characteristic of God is that He searches for those who are wayward.

→ Read Luke 15 in the following portions.

- Verses 1-7
- Verses 8-10
- Verses 11-24
- Verses 25-32

→ What things were lost? How were they found? What were the searchers' reactions?

Sometimes the church acts like the older brother in Luke 15:25-32.

→ How can our church guard against the attitudes of pride and selfishness shown by the older brother?

⟶ **Watch DVD session 2.**

Why do we love?

⟶ **Read Zephaniah 3:17:**

Yahweh your God is among you,
a warrior who saves.
He will rejoice over you with gladness.
He will bring you quietness with His love.
He will delight in you with shouts of joy.

Many have mischaracterized the Old Testament's presentation
of God as wrathful and angry.

⟶ **How does this verse present God?**

God's first call is for His people to be intimately related to Him.

⟶ **Read the following verses and identify God's common call
to the rebellious Israelites.**
  • **Isaiah 44:22**
  • **Jeremiah 24:7**
  • **Joel 2:12**
  • **Zechariah 1:3**
  • **Malachi 3:7**

⟶ **God's call in these verses:**

God wants rebellious people to return to Him.

⟶ **How does that fact affect the attitudes we hold toward the lost
in our community?**

The Son Was Willing to Die

During Jesus' earthly ministry He experienced both acceptance and rejection. Yet He continued to move toward the cross.

⟶ **Read John 5:19-24; 15:9-13 and explain how love played a role in Jesus' continued ministry.**

The words *dying* and *love* are not often placed together. Yet Christ's death is His ultimate expression of love on our behalf.

⟶ **Discuss what Christ's death means for the following.**

- **Our eternal destiny:**
- **Our victory over temptation:**
- **Our relationships with other believers:**
- **Our relationships with the lost:**

⟶ **Read 1 John 4:17-21:**

In this, love is perfected with us so that we may have confidence in the day of judgment, for we are as He is in this world. There is no fear in love; instead, perfect love drives out fear, because fear involves punishment. So the one who fears has not reached perfection in love. We love because He first loved us. If anyone says, "I love God," yet hates his brother, he is a liar. For the person who does not love his brother he has seen cannot love the God he has not seen. And we have this command from Him: The one who loves God must also love his brother.

As God has loved us, we are to love other people. Otherwise, verse 20 says we are liars.

→ Use the following list to discuss a few ways you and your church can be more loving.

- Caring for orphans
- Beginning a ministry to new immigrants
- Connecting with a missionary in another region of the world
- Doing home-improvement projects for the elderly
- Coaching teams in a local recreation league
- Beginning a Bible study in a nursing home
- Inviting neighbors to eat dinner in your home
- Helping a single mom with child care a few times a month
- Sending care packages to soldiers
- Intervening with a couple that is experiencing marital problems
- Confronting a friend about their sin
- Becoming involved in the local parent-teacher organization
- Other:

→ **Read Jesus' words in John 15:12-15:**

This is My command: Love one another as I have loved you. No one has greater love than this, that someone would lay down his life for his friends. You are My friends if you do what I command you. I do not call you slaves anymore, because a slave doesn't know what his master is doing. I have called you friends, because I have made known to you everything I have heard from My Father.

God is willing to accept us as friends rather than mere slaves.

→ **What does this say about the nature of God's love?**

The Spirit Is Willing to Teach and Convict

First Corinthians 2:6-16 teaches that the Holy Spirit is active in our lives.

⟶ **What does He do to aid us in our walk of faith?**

⟶ **Read John 16:7-11:**

I am telling you the truth. It is for your benefit that I go away, because if I don't go away the Counselor will not come to you. If I go, I will send Him to you. When He comes, He will convict the world about sin, righteousness, and judgment: About sin, because they do not believe in Me; about righteousness, because I am going to the Father and you will no longer see Me; and about judgment, because the ruler of this world has been judged.

⟶ **Why was it important for Christ to leave the earth after His resurrection?**

Conclusion

⟶ **What difference will knowing God's character and activity make in the way you seek to live missionally?**

⟶ **Close with prayer. Before the next group experience, read the daily devotions for week 2.**

WEEK 2

Our Missionary God

CITIZEN MISSIONARIES

Theologians have discussed, debated, preached, and written on the subject of God's kingdom for centuries. From the time of the first-century church until now, Christians have sought to balance the necessity of living in this world with the knowledge that our citizenship is somewhere else.

This understanding is reflected in the New Testament. In speaking about those who have rejected Christ, Paul wrote in Philippians 3:19-21:

> *Their end is destruction; their god is their stomach; their glory is in their shame. They are focused on earthly things, but our citizenship is in heaven, from which we also eagerly wait for a Savior, the Lord Jesus Christ. He will transform the body of our humble condition into the likeness of His glorious body, by the power that enables Him to subject everything to Himself.*

Again, in Ephesians 2:17-19 Paul wrote:

> *When the Messiah came, He proclaimed the good news of peace to you who were far away and peace to those who were near. For through Him we both have access by one Spirit to the Father. So then you are no longer foreigners and strangers, but fellow citizens with the saints, and members of God's household.*

What two images did Paul use to describe our identity as believers?

1. _____ _____ **with the saints**
2. _____ **of God's household**

Where is our true citizenship as believers?

To live missionally, we need to understand where our ultimate allegiance lies. Notice that I said "ultimate" because Scripture teaches that we are to be good earthly citizens to the extent that it does not interfere with our obedience to God's Word. Our eternal citizenship, however, is in God's kingdom. Therefore, we must be more concerned with the expansion of His rule and reign than with any earthly power.

Citizenship comes with privileges and responsibilities.

- We are privileged to be members of God's kingdom, which is victorious 100 percent of the time. God's sovereignty is indisputable. Otherwise, He would not be God.
- We are adopted into the King's family. Rather than serving as mere foot soldiers, we are blessed to have a royal crest over our heads.
- We have a personal relationship with our King.

Knowing such sublime truths makes me long for permanent entrance into the gates of God's city!

The responsibilities of kingdom citizenship are just as wonderful. As you studied in last week's devotionals, we serve as ambassadors for God's kingdom. Our citizenship is not sedentary; it is actively engaging the earthly kingdom. And let there be no mistaking that there is really only one other kingdom—the kingdom of darkness from which we were rescued and now seek to rescue others as well. †

Describe in your own words your responsibilities as a kingdom citizen.

DAY 1
The Father's Care

On that day it will be said to Jerusalem:
"Do not fear;
Zion, do not let your hands grow weak.
Yahweh your God is among you,
a warrior who saves.
He will rejoice over you with gladness.

He will bring you quietness with his love.
He will delight in you with shouts of joy."
I will gather those who have been driven
from the appointed festivals;
they will be a tribute from you
and a reproach on her.

ZEPHANIAH 3:16-18

Fathers are funny creatures. I can say that because I am one. We want to be both valorous and silly. The joys gained in fatherhood are found more often in the commonplace experiences of everyday life than in the dramatic moments that happen every so often.

The fatherhood of God is normally highlighted as a New Testament concept. But the Hebrew people of the Old Testament understood that God was not just the Judge of heaven. Life and breath descended from Him to all creation, and they were pleased to learn of His fatherhood over His people.

The Old Testament prophet Zephaniah denounced the rampant idolatry in Israel. His short book is filled with the dire consequences awaiting the Hebrews for their sin. But the final chapter provides a twinge of hope because of God's care for His people.

**Read Zephaniah 3:16-18 at the beginning of today's lesson.
What fatherly actions characterize God in this passage?**

These words promise God's presence, which brings salvation. If nothing else, fathers should *be there.* Our Heavenly Father's presence is not merely obligatory or supervisory. His presence makes a difference in our lives.

When Moses knew he would soon die and Joshua would be the new leader, he said to him:

> *Be strong and courageous, for you will go with this people into the land the* LORD *swore to give to their fathers. You will enable them to take possession of it. The* LORD *is the One who will go before you. He will be with you; He will not leave you or forsake you. Do not be afraid or discouraged (Deut. 31:7-8).*

What encouragement does this passage give to you as a missional Christian?

The strength and courage needed to participate in God's work is not found naturally within us. Rather, it comes from God's abiding presence in our lives.

Divine presence also brings about rest in our lives. Zephaniah 3:17 says, "He will bring you quietness with his love." Our earthly dads have some of that impact as well. When all seems to be unraveling, a father's presence allows us to rest. Feelings of anxiety and abandonment are replaced with a quiet camaraderie.

Our lives are filled with an endless amount of noise, some of it self-imposed. Often we find solace in a noisy background that drowns out the pressures of the day. Christians have the opportunity to find quietness and rest in the constant presence of the eternal God. Hope springs in our lives when we allow the Father to simply quiet us and hold us close.

And God sings a divine song over us. When my two sons were preschoolers, my wife and I often made up songs for them. In particular, we had a bathtime song that was a big hit our home. Although it was silly and meaningless, our joy was found not in composing it but in our children's enjoyment of it.

As Christians, we are rightly accustomed to singing songs of praise to God. Having God sing a song of joy over us seems backward. Yet just as earthly parents sing children to sleep with a quiet lullaby or wake them with a rousing song, God rejoices over His children with a joyful song.

God's character is the only constant in our lives. It is what we must rely on to work in His mission. And it is the retreat we need when the work is hard. As you work in the middle of God's mission, take time to retreat into His presence and find your rest in Him. It will be the precious place where God refreshes your soul with His joy. †

For some people, the image of a father is not a positive one. List ways God is the perfect Father to Christians.

Because God is present with us, how do His qualities empower us to work in His mission to save the lost and encourage the saved?

Spend time resting in your Father's arms. Be refreshed as you express your love for Him and let Him sing His song over you.

DAY 2
The Father's Jealousy

You must not bow down to them or worship them; for I, the LORD your God, am a jealous God, punishing the children for the fathers' sin, to the third and fourth generations of those who hate Me, but showing faithful love to a thousand generations of those who love Me and keep My commands.

EXODUS 20:5-6

As God gave Moses the Ten Commandments, He referred to Himself as a jealous God. When we are jealous, it is normally a sin. Someone buys a car we want or gets a promotion we think we earned. God, however, is jealous for righteous reasons. The praise that humankind would give to idols truly belongs to God. Exodus 34:14 highlights God's righteous jealousy: "Do not worship any other god, for the LORD, whose name is Jealous, is a jealous God" (NIV). God names Himself Jealous. In all Scripture jealousy is the only emotion God names Himself. Why is God jealous for His people?

God is jealous because He is our Creator, and He loves us. In great passion God pursued a people to call His own from among the nations. Abram became Abraham and the father of the Hebrews. God heard their cry when they were enslaved and snatched them from harm's way. In their covenant with the Lord, they promised to be faithful; and He sought to ensure that faithfulness. Time and time again when they sinned, He brought them discomfort so that they would reenter a faithful relationship with God. Our God loves His people so much that He will go to any length to reclaim us, bringing us back into a right-standing relationship with Him.

God is jealous for us because of His image in us. The careful hands that fashioned the universe also placed His image within us. When creating Adam, God set an echo of Himself in humanity that should be protected from the stain of sin. God's jealousy therefore has something to do with us but much more to do with Himself. God is rightfully jealous for His glory to be seen by the nations, and He wants us to reflect that glory. Psalm 72:19 says:

> May His glorious name be praised forever;
> the whole earth is filled with His glory.
> Amen and amen.

God is jealous for His character to be displayed and for humanity's soul to be redeemed. Our mission should reflect God's heart of jealous love. Paul wrote about his ministry to the early Christians of Corinth, "I am jealous over you with a godly jealousy, because I have promised you in marriage to one husband—to present a purec virgin to Christ" (2 Cor. 11:2). As we look out our front doors to a street filled with wayward hearts, we should cringe that God is not famous there. When we read reports of war, poverty, disease, and all forms of hopelessness, we should long for God's great heart to be known in those places.

Identify some places in *your* world that desperately need God's presence.

Yet we must also remember that He has given that task to the church. Ephesians 3:10 says, "This is so God's multi-faceted wisdom may now be made known through the church to the rulers and authorities in the heavens." As His church, we should urgently desire God's greatness to be displayed in us to the world. †

As you pray today, identify what your heart is jealous for in this life. Your love for God should be so great that you are jealous when anything else supersedes His place in your life. Identify idols in your life—things, activities, ambitions—that threaten to usurp God's place as Lord.

Your mission for others' hope should have within it a quality of jealousy for God's character to show through their redemption. Seek to imitate the character of our Heavenly Father, who is jealous for His glory and our good. Are you jealous for the unbelievers on the mission list you began in week 1 (p. 158)?

Review your mission list on page 158 and pray for those persons today.

DAY 3
Heroism

As the Father has loved Me, I have also loved you. Remain in My love. If you keep My commands you will remain in My love, just as I have kept My Father's commands and remain in His love. I have spoken these things to you so that My joy may be in you and your joy may be complete. This is My command: Love one another as I have loved you. No one has greater love than this, that someone would lay down his life for his friends.

JOHN 15:9-13

Like most children, I was fascinated by heroes. It's easy for most people to be caught up in the adventure-filled life of heroic battles and victories. But as we mature into adulthood, we leave behind the hope for heroism in our lives. Only soldiers, athletes, and firefighters seem to fill the role of hero in the eyes of adults.

In Christ we find the personification of heroism.

Identify some ways Jesus was the greatest hero of all time.

When others fled the dangers of Rome and religious legalism, Jesus remained faithful to the Father's mission to bring freedom to humankind. While the religious powers of the day warned Him to be silent, He stood with steady courage against human laws that condemned people's souls. Arrested and charged with crimes against the Roman Empire, Christ was asked whether He was the King. His resolute answer sealed His fate.

As God in flesh, Jesus was steadfast in the work that lay before Him in His own death. In John 15:9-13 He spoke of the type of heroism necessary for obedience to such a work: "As the Father has loved Me, I have also loved you. Remain in My love. If you keep My commands you will remain in My love, just as I have kept My Father's commands and remain in His love. I have spoken these things to you so that My joy may be in you and your joy may be complete. This is My command: Love one another as I have loved you. No one has greater love than this, that someone would lay down his life for his friends. "

When we consider the heroes of human history (and imagination), we seldom think of Christ. Yet look at His life. When everyone else was running away, He ran straight into the most important event in human history—the cross.

Who in your life especially needs to hear about Jesus' heroic actions?

Giving one's life on behalf of others seems to be an almost mythological tale reserved for soldiers on foreign soil. We find ourselves voiceless when such a story is told on the news. Jesus reminds us that dying for someone else requires "greater love" (v. 13). The sacrifice of life itself can be propelled only by a love that exceeds the obligatory care of others. Jesus had a greater love and was killed because of it.

The missional life calls for us to sacrifice, as Jesus sacrificed His life for us. Second Corinthians 4:10 teaches, "We always carry the death of Jesus in our body, so that the life of Jesus may also be revealed in our body." Hopefully, you and I will never face a death sentence for our profession of faith. But many in our world do. During a visit to the Middle East, I met men and women whose lives are constantly under the threat of death. One pastor in a rural town told us that whenever they have a baptism, they have persecution. Believers in militant countries meet secretly, are frequently arrested, and are executed outside the gaze of the modern media.

Would you sacrifice yourself for the cause of Christ? Chances are, you have asked that question of yourself. Moving away from that far end of the spectrum, perhaps we should also ask ourselves what sacrifices we can make now that are in line with God's mission. †

Review the mission list you began in week 1 (p. 158). Now is the time for you to be missional, revealing the life and truth of Jesus in your witnessing. Pray about the persons on your list and about your commitment to share Christ with them. Do you care enough about them to sacrifice your own self-interest and agenda?

How can you be an active friend in the lives of the unbelievers you know?

If you know very few lost persons, resolve to get out of your bubble, box, or subculture. Jesus did not die simply for you to live a safe life. He died for the eternal hope of your family, friends, neighbors, and coworkers. Today make the resolution of soul that you will begin to meet the lost persons in your life for whom the Son has heroically died. Identify some ways you can meet them.

DAY 4
The Passionate Missionary

Make your own attitude that of Christ Jesus, who, existing in the form of God, did not consider equality with God as something to be used for His own advantage. Instead He emptied Himself by assuming the form of a slave, taking on the likeness of men. And when He had come as a man in His external form, He humbled Himself by becoming obedient to the point of death—even to death on a cross.

PHILIPPIANS 2:5-8

Jesus cannot be relegated to any position lower than his true one—God and King. Yet He chose to humble himself for the incarnation. God the Son became the Son of Man to accomplish the task of redemption. He was the model, example, and perfection of missional living. Jesus humbly received the task from God the Father and fulfilled it perfectly.

One scene from the Gospels that displays the passion of Christ is found in John 2:12-25. Jesus had returned to Jerusalem for the Passover, one of Israel's most important religious festivals. But when He arrived at the temple, He found that it had been transformed into a shopping center.

Years earlier the temple officials had decided to begin offering money-exchange services to make it more convenient for worshipers to make offerings to God. Then people began selling animals for pilgrims to purchase as sacrifices to God. Over time abuses crept into the system. Animals with imperfections were sold and sacrificed even though they did not meet God's standards. Greedy money changers became more interested in profit than in providing a reasonable service for worshipers.

Describe the effect this situation must have had on people's efforts to worship God.

By Jesus' day all of the bartering had been moved into the Court of the Gentiles. Can you imagine what it would have been like for a Gentile who was seeking to worship and hear the message from the Scriptures? How debilitating of soul to know you mattered so little to the Jews that they were selling sheep and clanging coins where you hoped to worship. God's intention was to create a place where all could worship the Lord and learn about His holiness. Now it looked more like a three-ring circus.

Completely offended by this scene, Jesus did what any good missionary would have done in such a circumstance: He made a bullwhip and began clearing the temple. I don't recommend that you repeat Christ's actions; you are not God's Son, and you do not worship in the Jewish temple. But because He was perfect, His action was perfect.

What do you think motivated Jesus' forceful response?

The disciples, though probably speechless, were no doubt reminded of the psalmist's words "Zeal for your house has consumed me" (Ps. 69:9) when they saw Jesus whip people right out of the temple. Jesus showed Himself as the great, eternal missionary in His passion for two things—worship and people. In John 2:16 He declared, "Get these things out of here! Stop turning My Father's house into a marketplace!"

Jesus was clearing the way for worship and evangelism. The outer court, where the businessmen had set up shop, was the only location where Gentiles could come near to hear of God's mercy. Christ demanded that they have a clear path instead of one cluttered by the Hebrews' need for convenience.

Humans tend to seek paths of least resistance—even Christians. We like what we like, and we like to keep it that way. Jesus' actions are not a call for you to turn over the table where they sell CDs of your pastor's messages or to close down the church bookstore. Instead, we should evaluate whether our religious practices and patterns of worship are hindering lost people from encountering God. Like Jesus, are we passionate for the nations to worship God? †

Identify barriers you and your church have set up that keep people from hearing the gospel and submitting to Christ. Examples might range from an unwritten dress code to judgmental attitudes toward ethical behavior.

What evidence from your life suggests that you are passionate to reach others for Christ?

What evidence shows that your church is passionate about reaching the lost?

DAY 5
Remembering All

*The Counselor, the Holy Spirit—the Father will send Him in My name—
will teach you all things and remind you of everything I have told you.*
JOHN 14:26

God's love can never be measured, but He shows it to us in a myriad of ways. Our study—or any study—can touch on only a few of them. It will take a lifetime of dedication to the Word and prayer to simply begin understanding the ways of God. For this reason we should understand the Holy Spirit's role in our lives. Beyond the Son's act of redemption on our behalf, the Holy Spirit's work in our lives demonstrates God's love to us and teaches us how to show His love to others.

I praise God for the Holy Spirit's presence in my life. He is the indwelling presence of the eternal God in the life of a mortal man. I am only earth and dust. He is love itself. God the Holy Spirit has come down to live within me.

As Jesus spent His last few hours with His closest followers, He taught at length about the work of the Holy Spirit. In John 14:26 He said, "The Counselor, the Holy Spirit—the Father will send Him in My name—will teach you all things and remind you of everything I have told you."

What two things did Jesus say the Holy Spirit would do for us?

1.

2.

A friend of mine asks the congregation the same thing each time He teaches this passage: "And what is included in everything?" And they answer, "Everything." God's love does not reach halfway on anything. Aware of our helpless state without His aid, the entire Trinity comes to our rescue; and the Spirit of God is sent for our benefit.

The Spirit's role is not a benign presence that keeps life on an even keel. With power and insight He teaches us everything we need to know to be blissfully obedient to God's directives and mission. Some believers resist this truth because their experience does not reflect Christ's teaching. But who is at fault? God does not change, so it must be our dull hearing and hardened hearts that do not perceive the Spirit's teaching.

Paul taught the Corinthian church the Spirit's role: "We have not received the spirit of the world, but the Spirit who comes from God, so that we may understand what has been freely given to us by God. We also speak these things, not in words taught by human wisdom, but in those taught by the Spirit, explaining spiritual things to spiritual people" (1 Cor. 2:12-13). Our cities today are much like immoral Corinth, and our churches are prone to the same weaknesses as the Corinthian believers. God sees our obvious needs and teaches us through His indwelling presence.

Think of all the lessons you have learned about God and about life in Christ as you have studied Scripture and heard it proclaimed and taught publicly. The Holy Spirit has personally activated each element of truth you know about God in your life. Without Him your Christian life would have remained in infancy.

How have you recently experienced the Holy Spirit's work in your life was you have shown God's love to others?

Because God is on mission in our world, we are to follow Him in it. The Holy Spirit is always available to teach us about our mission and to help us apply God's Word in carrying out that mission to the lost. †

What questions do you have about your mission to reach the lost? List things you want to learn more about in the areas of evangelism, discipleship, God's character, and God's kingdom.

How would fully understanding the issues you listed aid you in witnessing to the lost and serving those in need?

What will you do to make yourself available to the Holy Spirit's instruction in these areas?

SESSION 3

Our Missional Endeavor

SESSION GOAL

You will examine Jesus' expectation
that a church make disciples,
and you will consider your role
in this vital ministry.

Missional Checkup

→ **In day 2 you read about God's jealousy for His children.
How did you adjust your perspective to have a godly jealousy
for others' spiritual growth this week?**

→ **How did you seek to carry the gospel to your lost friends
this week?**

The Purpose of the Church

→ Why does the church exist? Give as many one-word answers as possible.

→ Identify ways your church excels in these areas.

→ What could your study group do over the next few weeks to encourage your church to excel in missional living?

→ Which one of the following do you understand to be the central work of your church and why?

- Teaching personal devotion to Christ
- Evangelizing the community and the world
- Worshiping together
- Encouraging other church members
- Serving people outside the church
- Being the conscience of culture
- Other:

→ Watch DVD segment 3 and answer these questions.

In what sense do Christians need to become countercultural?

How can believers best serve other people?

→ **Read Matthew 28:18-20, the Great Commission:**

Jesus came near and said to them, "All authority has been given to Me in heaven and on earth. Go, therefore, and make disciples of all nations, baptizing them in the name of the Father and of the Son and of the Holy Spirit, teaching them to observe everything I have commanded you. And remember, I am with you always, to the end of the age."

→ **According to this passage, what is the central reason for the church's existence?**

Presence and Power

The Great Commission begins and ends with Jesus' statement about His presence with believers.

→ **How does His promise affect the way we work to fulfill the Great Commission?**

→ **Read 2 Corinthians 4:7:**

We have this treasure in clay jars, so that this extraordinary power may be from God and not from us.

→ **Give a personal testimony of God's work in your life that displayed His power in you.**

Going

Jesus told the apostles to go.

→ **What are some ways we can go more effectively into our community? Name places in your town or city where there is not a sufficient gospel witness.**

→ **Read Romans 10:14-15:**

How can they call on Him they have not believed in? And how can they believe without hearing about Him? And how can they hear without a preacher? And how can they preach unless they are sent? As it is written: How beautiful are the feet of those who announce the gospel of good things!

Clearly, verbal witnessing is part of missional living.

→ **Refer to your mission list on page 158. Share the first names of those you feel most urgently need to receive your verbal witness. Pause and pray for them.**

→ **Read God's call to Paul in Acts 16:6-10:**

They went through the region of Phrygia and Galatia and were prevented by the Holy Spirit from speaking the message in Asia. When they came to Mysia, they tried to go into Bithynia, but the Spirit of Jesus did not allow them. So, bypassing Mysia, they came down to Troas. During the night a vision appeared to Paul: A Macedonian man was standing and pleading with him, "Cross over to Macedonia and help us!" After he had seen the vision, we immediately made efforts to set out for Macedonia, concluding that God had called us to evangelize them.

Paul heard a call to a place and a people.

→ **Discuss the following phrases from the passage.**

- "To Macedonia." In what place is our church called to work?

- "Help us!" What help was Paul to give?

- "We immediately made efforts." What is the role of immediate obedience in missional living?

Making Disciples

Jesus commanded that we are to "make disciples" (Matt. 28:19). Making disciples of unbelievers involves more than getting them to pray a salvation prayer.

→ **List some ways your church could help new believers grow spiritually.**

→ **Share your baptism story.**

- How old were you?
- What did you have to understand before you were baptized?
- What were the reactions of your friends?
- How can your baptism play a role in your witnessing now?

For years the church has separated evangelism and discipleship. Evangelistic training is held during one hour and discipleship groups at other times.

⟶   What can we do to bring these elements back together?

⟶   What basic lessons do new believers need to get on a path of missional living?

Passion for the Lost

God's passion for the lost is evident throughout Scripture.

⟶   Identify Scriptures that illustrate this truth and discuss their application to the lost people you know. Here are some examples: Eden, delivering the Hebrews from Egypt, Isaiah's prophecies to the nations, tax collectors befriended by Jesus, Peter's visiting Cornelius's home, Paul's conversion.

Whether or not we go out as missional believers depends on our love for God, but our love for the lost also plays a part.

⟶   Discuss the differences between the Old Testament prophet Jonah and the New Testament apostle Paul. Specifically talk about their degree of passion for the people God called them to reach.

Conclusion

⟶   Pray that the Lord will increase your passion for the lost so that it will mirror His. Before the next group experience, read the daily devotions for week 3.

WEEK 3

Our Missional Endeavor

RECONCILING EVANGELISM AND DISCIPLE MAKING

Missional living is deeply concerned with the truth. Jesus stated in John 14:6 that He is the truth. The Bible is God's true revelation of Himself to humankind. Paul encouraged Timothy to understand the usefulness of God's Word (see 2 Tim. 3:14-17). And for us, God's truth is the best news we will ever hear. In fact, the Greek word translated *gospel* literally means *good news*.

As we work in God's mission, the purposes have often been expressed as evangelizing the lost and discipling the saved. It is time for us to reclaim these ideas as one singular purpose of making disciples of all nations (see Matt. 28:19).

As Jude wrote to the early church, he encouraged believers to stand up for the faith and warned them of the false doctrines infiltrating the church. Toward the end of his short letter, he summarized our work this way:

> *Remember what was predicted by the apostles of our Lord Jesus Christ; they told you, "In the end time there will be scoffers walking according to their own ungodly desires." These people create divisions and are unbelievers, not having the Spirit. But you, dear friends, as you build yourselves up in your most holy faith and pray in the Holy Spirit, keep yourselves in the love of God, expecting the mercy of our Lord Jesus Christ for eternal life. Have mercy on those who doubt; save others by snatching them from the fire; have mercy on others but with fear, hating even the garment defiled by the flesh (Jude 17-23).*

Missional living combines the ideas of growing up and reaching out. As in Jude's day, we have scoffers in the world today—those who doubt with angst in their hearts. Yet we are not to be soiled by their corruption. Instead, we are to mature in our faith, even in the midst of a pagan culture. We have every opportunity to grow stronger in our faith, and we should.

Check the opportunities you have as a believer to grow in your faith.

- Small-group Bible study
- Personal quiet time
- Corporate worship
- Private worship
- Fellowship with believers
- Ministry to others
- Discipleship courses
- Other:

From the previous list, what would you like to begin doing that would help you grow spiritually?

Our spiritual maturation should result in evangelistic fervor. On the heels of Jude's admonition to grow up, he quickly tells us to reach out. We are to show mercy to the doubters and urgency to those in eternal jeopardy. Missional living centers on the truth of the good news. It focuses on the lost friend and the saved brother. Our task, as Jesus defined it, is the ministry of disciple making. As we evangelize, we should do it with the goal of leading someone through all the great truths God has given us. As we disciple, we should do it with the goal of leading other believers to share their faith. As you press forward in missional living, make it your priority to produce fully functioning disciples of Christ. †

Do your efforts to grow in Christ lead you to reach out to unbelievers? If not, how does your personal spiritual development need to change in order to focus more on sharing the good news?

DAY 1
The Great Commission

Jesus came near and said to them, "All authority has been given to Me in heaven and on earth. Go, therefore, and make disciples of all nations, baptizing them in the name of the Father and of the Son and of the Holy Spirit, teaching them to observe everything I have commanded you. And remember, I am with you always, to the end of the age."

MATTHEW 28:18–20

I was taught the Great Commission many years ago. When I was a child, Jesus' command seemed to be something reserved for pastors and missionaries. But as I grew in my faith, I realized its application to my own life in Christ. Jesus had spoken to the early believers in Matthew 28, but He was also speaking to me.

The Great Commission is a tipping-point command for believers today. Christ's words press us over the edge from the church as fellowship to the church as missionaries. And it comes from His seat of power. When Jesus stood on the mountain to deliver the commission, He was not speaking as a Jewish rabbi or a traveling philosopher. He spoke to them—and us—as the true King of glory. His rightful claim to hold all authority in heaven and on earth (see v. 18) leaves us in no position to bargain about our obedience.

How would submitting to Christ's authority in your life change each of the following areas?

Your obedience to His commands:

Your use of time and money:

Your service:

Your desire to be on mission:

Missional living has a point. Ultimately, it is to glorify God, just as everything in eternity should bring Him glory. Missional living has a practical point as well—to distribute the gospel to people who do not believe in Christ and to see them follow Him. To that end, missional living must be done at all times and in all places.

Sending official missionaries around the world is one way we "make disciples of all nations" (v. 19). When a couple hears God's call to take the gospel to South America, we applaud them, pray for them, and let them go. But the word *go* is quite important for us as well. It literally means *as you are going*. Equating mission work with foreign places has always been a mistake. God's expectation is that we make disciples as we are going to work, home, school, and the local ball field. It is applicable and critical for every arena of life. We do not have the luxury of waiting for another missionary to move into our neighborhood. We are the missionaries.

Have you been on mission to someone lately?

If so, describe what you did or said.

But the Great Commission is not just about going. We must aim for specific results—making disciples, including them in the church, and teaching them to obey. I fear we have stopped short on much of this work. We sometimes excel at evangelistic excitement. But we do very little to engage people in conversations that would lead them over the threshold of faith. We love it when people join the church. But we like to leave it to the pastor to convince them to show their salvation through baptism. We love it when people lead discipleship studies for our church. But we have not yet found a new Christian whom we can personally lead toward spiritual maturity.

If you have led someone to the Lord, identify a next step you need to take to encourage their spiritual growth.

The bottom line is that we are to fulfill the Great Commission. God was not speaking to a different class of believers. He was talking to you and me. †

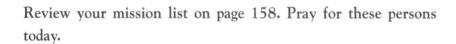

Review your mission list on page 158. Pray for these persons today.

What are some ways you can actively take the gospel with you as you go about your normal activities? Check all that apply.
- Verbally witnessing
- Aiding new Christians
- Inviting someone to attend a church service
- Serving someone who has a need
- Other:

DAY 2

Your Macedonia

During the night a vision appeared to Paul: A Macedonian man was standing and pleading with him, "Cross over to Macedonia and help us!" After he had seen the vision, we immediately made efforts to set out for Macedonia, concluding that God had called us to evangelize them.

ACTS 16:9-10

Have you ever been puzzled about what to do next in God's kingdom? I have. We all experience moments or days when we want to be obedient to what God has for us to do next, but we simply cannot see what it is.

Paul and his companions had the same experience. In Acts 16 they tried going in several directions, but God hampered their progress at every turn. Finally, Paul found out what they were to do next (see vv. 9-10). When Paul received the Macedonian call, it gave him direction. After other attempts at ministry, he now knew his next destination.

Why is direction important in missional living?

Having a destination is comforting in missional ministry. The feeling that we are flailing about in ministry is frustrating. Constant expenditures of energy without the assurance that we are fulfilling God's will drain us, exhaust the church, and bleed hope dry.

Where is God sending you? The answer could be as simple as the places you visit every day. Be careful not to complicate seeking God's will.

Perhaps where you are is where God wants you to be. I live in a community to which most people have moved from other locations. I remind our church members that God has sent them here not just to live but also to be missional. They were looking for a nice house in a nice neighborhood near a nice school, but God was orchestrating a mission field for them to live in and be His witnesses. He was connecting them to a specific people He wanted them to be involved with.

The Macedonian man's plea in Paul's vision was "Help us!" (v. 9).

Reread verses 9-10. What did the Macedonians need?

We make choices each day as to whether we will help people for Kingdom purposes. Our help should always point the lost toward Christ. When it's all over, people should be able to say that you and I presented Jesus to them. Making cookies for a neighbor or helping a coworker with a project portrays Christ's kind character in us. But if our help stops there, our love for them has fallen woefully short of Christ's standard. The great help we can offer is a vision of Christ's work on the cross for their eternal salvation and for a personal relationship with God.

Think about persons on your mission list (p. 158) with whom you are cultivating relationships. Identify any with whom you need to go ahead and share the gospel.

When Paul knew it to be God's will, he "immediately made efforts to set out" (v. 10). Paul was always on go. Hesitation seemed to be a foreign concept to him. He was excited to be on a missional endeavor with God! But when God calls us to go on mission, why do we dawdle like children called to a plateful of broccoli for dinner? Our obedience has waned. Why?

- Embarrassment
- Insecurity
- Discouragement from past ministry attempts
- Desire to fit in with the crowd
- Fear of rejection

In the previous list, check any reasons that are delaying you when God has called you to go on mission.

Paul seemed to have none of these hang-ups. When asked to leap into Macedonia, he went. Once there, he searched for people with whom to share the good news. He was later imprisoned but thrived anyway.

We should react as Paul did to our current assignment from the Father. The neighborhood we live in, the job we work in, the parent-teacher organization we attend, and the parks we play in—these are our Macedonia! †

Identify the places God is sending you at present.

Pray and ask the Father to make you sensitive to any specific call in the places you go. What do you sense God is calling you to do?

Renew your love for God in prayer so that your obedience will be immediate and complete. Also ask Him to reshape your view of ministry so that the help you provide points the way to Jesus, lasting throughout all eternity.

DAY 3

Tantrums and Triumphs

I speak the truth in Christ—I am not lying; my conscience is testifying to me with the Holy Spirit—that I have intense sorrow and continual anguish in my heart. For I could almost wish to be cursed and cut off from the Messiah for the benefit of my brothers, my own flesh and blood.

They are Israelites, and to them belong the adoption, the glory, the covenants, the giving of the law, the temple service, and the promises. The ancestors are theirs, and from them, by physical descent, came the Messiah, who is God over all, praised forever. Amen.

ROMANS 9:1-5

Everyone has certain responsibilities we fulfill simply because we must. For me, it's mowing the yard. I ignore, delay, and avoid yard work as long as I can. It must be attended to, but I simply don't enjoy it. Other people gain great satisfaction from yard work, so they look forward to the heat, the sweat, and the dirt. Where I see an hour of torture, they see a day of accomplishment.

Our perspective of missionary work can be just as varied. Some believers can't imagine themselves doing it, while others are on standby 24/7.

The Old Testament prophet Jonah was not ready to do the missionary work God assigned to him. After God first approached him, Jonah actually ran away, like a child running away from home. But when he discovered in the stomach of a fish that someone can't hide from God, he relented and traveled to Nineveh, the place of God's missionary calling for him. After he finally delivered God's message to the people of Nineveh, they all repented. Here is Jonah's response.

Jonah was greatly displeased and became furious. He prayed to the LORD: "Please, LORD, isn't this what I said while I was still in my own country? That's why I fled toward Tarshish in the first place. I knew that You are a merciful and compassionate God, slow to become angry, rich in faithful love, and One who relents from sending disaster. And now, LORD, please take my life from me, for it is better for me to die than to live" (Jonah 4:1-3).

That's right. God spared his life, he preached in Nineveh, and the people in that city repented before God. Yet Jonah sulked. In the face of deity, he sat in a huff wishing God had destroyed Nineveh.

Why do you think Jonah reacted this way?

Jonah's tantrum is not completely foreign to us. We must admit that at times we hope sinners in our day will receive judgment from God. Like Jonah, we know God is filled with gracious compassion; but we sometimes wish He would smite with fire rather than deliver with love. Jonah wished this enemy nation would receive an eternal judgment that would further vindicate his own people, Israel. He wanted God to conquer Nineveh. Oddly enough, God wanted to conquer Nineveh as well, only God wished to do so by their repentance rather than by His furious wrath.

Have you ever reacted the way Jonah did? If so, why?

Fast-forward to a new millennium, and we find the apostle Paul writing to the church in Rome. He was teaching a church under the heel of the empire's power to live with proper doctrine and pure lives. The church in Rome had obviously split with the religious system of the Jewish people and had stayed at odds with them. Our flesh cries out for friends under oppression to be publicly vindicated and our enemies to be humiliated. But in contrast to Jonah's tantrum, Paul triumphed over the natural man's desires.

Reread Romans 9:1-5 on page 71. Paul said he wished he could be cursed for the sake of his brothers. Why do you think he would say that?

Our high-school English teachers taught us about hyperbole, an exaggeration used to make a point (like "I'm so tired, I could sleep for a month"). Paul employed such a figure of speech in this passage. Theologically, he knew believers could not forfeit or lose their salvation. It is impossible for them to be "cut off from the Messiah" (v. 3). Paul was expressing his passion, just as Jonah had expressed his. Paul grieved that those who had crucified Jesus didn't recognize him as the Messiah, while Jonah had grieved that fire wasn't falling from heaven to obliterate Nineveh's people. When you think about the lost, do you desire their repentance or their judgment? †

Consider the judgment awaiting those without Christ. Read the following passages and record characteristics of hell.

Matthew 13:47-50:

Matthew 22:13:

Luke 16:22-28:

With this picture of eternal judgment in mind, look at your mission list on page 158. Identify anyone you would consider an enemy.

Do you genuinely desire their repentance, or would you rather let God judge them?

Diligently pray for the lost persons you know and ask the Lord to give you the desire and opportunity to share the gospel today with someone who is in imminent danger of judgment.

DAY 4

A New Shepherd

"This is what the Lord GOD says: See, I Myself will search for My flock and look for them. As a shepherd looks for his sheep on the day he is among his scattered flock, so I will look for My flock. I will rescue them from all the places where they have been scattered on a cloudy and dark day. I will bring them out from the peoples, gather them from the countries, and bring them into their own land. I will shepherd them on the mountains of Israel, in the ravines, and in all the inhabited places of the land. I will tend them with good pasture, and their grazing place will be on Israel's lofty mountains. There they will lie down in a good grazing place; they will feed in rich pasture on the mountains of Israel. I will tend My flock and let them lie down." This is the declaration of the Lord GOD. "I will seek the lost, bring back the strays, bandage the injured, and strengthen the weak, but I will destroy the fat and the strong. I will shepherd them with justice."

EZEKIEL 34:11-16

In Ezekiel 34 God spoke out against the shepherds of His people. Those who were supposed to lead, tend to, and defend the people of Israel had miserably failed in their assignment. Instead of making the sheep their first priority, they had cared only for themselves: "Woe to the shepherds of Israel, who have been feeding themselves! Shouldn't the shepherds feed their flock?" (Ezek. 34:2).

Christians today have something in common with the leaders of Israel: our missional task is to care for people, not ourselves. Each day we should carefully survey our sphere of influence for those who are in need, those who are wandering away, and those who are attacked by interlopers in the flock. Because God found the leaders of Ezekiel's day in such a poor state,

He declared that He would personally rescue the flock (see Ezek. 34:10). Then He described a true shepherd's work. Read again the passage at the beginning of today's lesson.

How is Jesus the Good Shepherd to you?

Though there is much to learn from the entire chapter, let's focus on the work of a good shepherd in verse 16.

Rescuing strays. Are you a parent with a wayward teenager? Perhaps you are a supervisor with an out-of-control employee. Or do you have a friend who is an alcoholic? Among your family and friends, some are lost and have gone astray. Maybe you have realized that no one else is attempting to reach them. So here is the proverbial million-dollar question: Will you go after that person?

Searching for the lost takes time, and bringing home a stray is messy business. People's sinful choices cause a lot of problems. That's why we rarely see people accepting wayward friends back into our circle of friendship. But God said part of His work is bringing back strays, so our mission must be the same. It is time for us to go out looking for our lost friends.

Examine your misson list on page 158. Record the name of someone who has gone astray and needs you to go after them.

Aiding the injured. Once you reconnect with someone who is lost, don't think your part in God's plan is over. Take the person to worship at church. Introduce them to the pastor. Get them involved in a Bible study group or Sunday School class. Missional living calls for personal interaction.

Verse 16 depicts the God of creation stooping down to bandage the wounded. The Almighty is personally involved to give strength to the weak. We are called to no less. And God's love within us should compel such a response to the one in need. As you look at the life of the friend who is marred by sin and injured by yielding to temptation, view them through the eternal lens through which God sees. He is a loving Shepherd who deeply cares for errant sheep.

Examine your mission list on page 158. Record the name of someone who is wounded.

Exercising just leadership. The last phrase in verse 16 calls for leadership that is fair-minded. God said, "I will shepherd them with justice." To understand the great need for justice among His people, read Ezekiel 34 in its entirety.

The leaders of the day had cared only for themselves. These stray shepherds had trampled the people and their needs underfoot. God was bringing justice back to a flock that had been left to the whims of the enemies. Like sheep at the mercy of wolves, Israel feared the wild beasts that would enslave them. As we live missionally, those we love should sense a certain valor in our leadership. As Paul wrote to young Timothy about leaders within the church, "This saying is trustworthy: 'If anyone aspires to be an overseer, he desires a noble work'" (1 Tim. 3:1).

In his shepherding work, God is able to work with compassion and justice while disregarding neither. Make sure your missional endeavors reflect these qualities as well. †

Examine your mission list on page 158. Record the name of someone who needs compassionate justice.

Name one action you will take to be a shepherd in someone's life.

DAY 5
Your Story

†—————————————————→

Today's devotional will be significantly different. Use your time with the Lord to recall and record Scriptures, people, circumstances, and God's promptings that led you to salvation. This activity will prepare you to share a clear account of how you were saved. As you live a missional life, you will find numerous opportunities to share all or part of your story to illustrate what God has done for you and what He can do for others.

You may write your story as a narrative or simply list the factors that led you to confess Christ as Savior and Lord. Here are a few suggestions. †

Who are the people who witnessed to you?

What Scripture passages helped you understand the gospel?

What circumstances showed you the need to repent and believe?

Describe the scene when you repented of your sins and placed your faith in Christ for salvation.

How has your life changed since you were born again?

How does knowing the great salvation you have received motivate you to share it with others?

Making a Missional Impact

GROUP EXPERIENCE

SESSION GOAL

You will discover that God created you
to make an incredible impact for His
kingdom, and you will consider ways
you can start making a difference.

Missional Checkup

→ Talk about a place you discovered to be your Macedonia this
week (the place where God is calling you to take the gospel).

→ When you wrote your testimony in day 5, what was one detail
that was particularly meaningful?

→ Discuss one witnessing experience you had or missed this week.

Contending for the Faith

→ Read Jude 3:

Dear friends, although I was eager to write you about our common salvation, I found it necessary to write and exhort you to contend for the faith that was delivered to the saints once for all.

Standing up for the faith is necessary but can become argumentative.

→ **Discuss common objections people give to becoming a Christian and how you can answer them from Scripture.**

→ **Watch DVD session 4 and answer these questions.**

How do believers contend for the faith?

What does it mean to contextualize the gospel?

→ **As you witness in your sphere of influence, what do you anticipate will be the greatest misconceptions about the church?**

→ **What biblical truths do you need to understand better to share your faith with unbelievers?**

→ **What could your group or church do to help bring better understanding of these truths?**

Jesus often dealt with detractors, but He never allowed His character to be compromised.

→ **List some of Jesus' detractors.**

→ **Identify ways Jesus' righteousness showed through when he responded to these detractors.**

→ **What are some distractions you deal with when contending for the faith?**

Eternal Life

→ **Read Jesus' words in John 3:34-36:**

God sent Him, and He speaks God's words, since He gives the Spirit without measure. The Father loves the Son and has given all things into His hands. The one who believes in the Son has eternal life, but the one who refuses to believe in the Son will not see life; instead, the wrath of God remains on him.

→ **How did love motivate Jesus to verbalize the Father's message?**

→ **How should love change the way we communicate to people who do not know Christ?**

Throughout history the church has properly highlighted that there is an eternal destination for every person—heaven or hell.

→ **Discuss Jesus' definition of *eternal life* in John 17:1-5.**

Becoming All Things

→ **Read Paul's words in 1 Corinthians 9:19-23:**

Although I am free from all people, I have made myself a slave to all, in order to win more people. To the Jews I became like a Jew, to win Jews; to those under the law, like one under the law—though I myself am not under the law—to win those under the law. To those who are outside the law, like one outside the law—not being outside God's law, but under the law of Christ—to win those outside the law. To the weak I became weak, in order to win the weak. I have become all things to all people, so that I may by all means save some. Now I do all this because of the gospel, that I may become a partner in its benefits.

→ **What are some ways churches behave that erect unnecessary barriers to understanding the meaning of the gospel message?**

→ **When you began attending church, what were some barriers to your understanding of the Christian life? You might discuss practices, worship styles, cliques, vocabulary, and so on.**

→ **If your church sent a family to serve as missionaries to a foreign country, how would they need to change in order to work in that country? Apply this question to a particular nation.**

Understanding our own culture is critical to communicating the message of Christ in an understandable way.

→ **Discuss the characteristics of your community. Consider economics, average family type, industries, education, subcultures, and pastimes.**

→ **How will these details affect the way you make disciples?**

To communicate the gospel in a contextualized format, we must choose to be around people who need to hear it.

→ **How can you begin to involve yourself more intentionally with the lost in your community?**

Conclusion

First Corinthians 9:23 says, "I do all this because of the gospel, that I may become a partner in its benefits."

→ **Discuss ways clearly communicating the gospel benefits Christians.**

→ **Close with prayer. Before the next group experience, read the daily devotions for week 4.**

WEEK 4

Making a Missional Impact

Why Contextualization Is Important

Once upon a time everyone knew what you meant when you spoke of the gospel, the Bible, Jesus, and church. Our American culture had a more singular profile then. But our country has always been the great melting pot of many nations and cultures. The inevitable result is a multicultural society.

I grew up in Birmingham during the 1970s and '80s. Almost everyone in my neighborhood was a Protestant. It was rare for me to meet another child who was a Roman Catholic. The mission field definitely felt far away.

Now the veil has been pulled back, and it is easy for us to see the broad spectrum that makes up our culture. Pastors, Bible study teachers, church planters, chaplains, and everyday Christians can no longer assume that others understand what we mean when we speak about the truths of Scripture. The *who* around us has changed, and our nation has been transformed into a vast mission field.

How has your community changed during the time you have lived there?

What barriers exist to the communication of the gospel in your community?

Ed Stetzer often says, "The how of ministry is often determined by the who, when, and where of culture." Have no doubt: the message of the gospel is not to be changed. It is an eternal message. Because of its timeless nature the gospel operates with equal power in all times and cultures.

Each generation of believers faces the temptation to create a subculture rather than to reach into their culture. Too often we have retreated from the world rather than engage it with the hope of the gospel. In retreating, we have shown antipathy toward the world and have lost our concern for their eternal destiny.

Mark the continuum to indicate the degree to which your church is engaging lost people with the truth of the gospel.

Retreat	Indifference	Intentional engagement

To love as God loves, we must go into the world. His example is clear in John 1:14, which teaches that God put on flesh and came to live in our neighborhood. While calling for faith and repentance, Jesus lived on our turf, spoke our language, wore our clothing, and ate our food. His very coming was an illustration of communicating the message of salvation in an understandable manner.

Making it understandable—that's the point of contextualization. From the early days of the Hebrew people until today, God has raised up mediating voices for His message. In Exodus 19:6 he said to Israel, "You will be My kingdom of priests and My holy nation." In Revelation 1:6 John told the believers scattered about the Roman Empire that God "made us a kingdom, priests to His God and Father." It is our duty to carry His message to those who are separated from Him. †

Define *contextualization* in your own words.

DAY 1
Religious People

I assure you: Unless someone is born again, he cannot see the kingdom of God.
JOHN 3:3

Once Jesus met a man with an impeccable religious heritage. The Bible identifies him as "a man from the Pharisees named Nicodemus, a ruler of the Jews" (John 3:1). More insight is given about Nicodemus in verse 10, where Jesus described him as Israel's teacher. As a participant in the Sanhedrin (the ruling council), Nicodemus in effect taught other teachers. It would be natural for such a highly religious man to feel assured of God's favor. Yet with all his religious clout, it was Nicodemus who sought Jesus. Apparently, something was missing in his life.

Why do you think Nicodemus sought Jesus even though he was a religious man?

Today missional believers face a religious culture. We must learn to contend with the formality of some and the intellectual gymnastics of others. Each day we meet with people who identify themselves with religious titles:
- "I'm Jewish."
- "My family is Roman Catholic."
- "We are Muslims."
- "I like Zen Buddhism."
- "Lately I've become …"

What are some non-Christian religions that are practiced in your community?

What do you think they offer that attracts people to them?

To belong is a powerful human desire that often leads generations of a family to commit to a religious structure. The commitments by one generation often lead to an identity for succeeding generations. The powerful desire to belong gives us insight into how we can present Christ to religious people.

In order to speak with others about the gospel, we need to understand the religious grid through which they see the world and eternity. After all, you will converse with a Jewish person differently than you will with a Mormon. As you pray about friends who are outside the faith, ask the Holy Spirit to give you understanding about how these friends think about God, eternity, and sin.

When Jesus met Nicodemus in the middle of the night, religious heritage was the starting point for their conversation. As a Jewish man with a great heritage, Nicodemus considered himself safely favored by God. However, Jesus immediately questioned that assumption: "I assure you: Unless someone is born again, he cannot see the kingdom of God" (John 3:3). The symbol of being born again certainly communicates the need for a new life to us today. But for Nicodemus, it would have also represented the shortcoming of his lineage. To be a pureblooded Hebrew signified easy access to God's eternal kingdom.

What approach to sharing the gospel would you take with friends whose religious identity is based on their family's heritage?

It was necessary for Jesus to separate Nicodemus from the family association so that he would see himself standing alone in need of God's redemptive work. In order for you to contend and contextualize, you will need to understand someone's religious background and then to help him or her separate from it. Separation may come easily if they see hypocrisy or contradictions in their faith tradition. It will nevertheless prove difficult for many to give up the religion of their parents and grandparents. In living missionally, I have dealt with people of various backgrounds who felt they would betray their families if they walked away from Judaism, Catholicism, and other religious backgrounds.

In dealing with a man knowledgeable of religious philosophy, Jesus spoke philosophically. He engaged Nicodemus with issues of the Spirit of God, prophecy in Moses' actions, truth, light, and darkness. I find that people are ready to speak about their religious heritage, and many of them are ready for something different or new. But to gain those opportunities, we need to be prepared. Listen closely as you build relationships with unbelievers. As you learn about their religious heritage and thoughts, God will make you sensitive to points at which they lack understanding about the gospel and how it can answer the shortcomings of their religious understanding of eternity. †

Look at your mission list (p. 158). Select two who are religious but are not Christians. List their names below. Beside each name identify two things:
1. Barriers their religious beliefs would pose to the gospel
2. How you would try to influence them, including Scriptures you would use

Pray for God to give you wisdom to know how to effectively share the gospel with these persons.

DAY 2
Guilty People

The woman said to Him, "I know that Messiah is coming" (who is called Christ). "When He comes, He will explain everything to us."
JOHN 4:25

John 3 revealed that Jesus had a common human ancestry with Nicodemus—the nation and religion of the Israelites. The story is quite the opposite in John 4, in which Jesus met the anonymous Samaritan woman at the well. In Jesus' example we discover some practical approaches to take with the lost.

Plan intentional meetings. For me, one of the great statements made in this account is one that is barely there. John 4:4 says, "He had to travel through Samaria." By the cultural norms of Jesus' day, this action was wrong on its face value. The Hebrew people considered Samaritans culturally unclean and avoided contact with them. Therefore, Israelites traveled around Samaria. Jesus, however, was not one to fear outsiders. He made it a point to meet them. Think of the "sinners and tax collectors" (Mark 2:16) with whom He associated. Beyond traveling through Samaria, Jesus broke down other cultural norms by speaking to a woman—and a Samaritan woman at that!

We should take up Jesus' mode of operation in making a missional impact. We must intentionally go to where lost people are. It would have been personally comfortable and socially acceptable for Jesus to wait in Jerusalem for all sinners to come hear Him speak. But knowing they would not, He intentionally traveled to where outsiders lived, worked, and suffered in their guilt.

What acquaintances on your mission list (p. 158) could you intentionally engage in a deeper friendship?

What intentional action do you need to take to go where these persons are?

Start with everyday subjects. "I don't know what to say" is a common reason Christians give for not sharing the gospel. The knot in your stomach betrays an unnecessary fear. Instead of worrying about what to say, follow Jesus' example and talk about whatever is close at hand. While visiting the woman at the well, He used the example of water, a common necessity. Jesus could have spoken on the intricate nature of water's molecular makeup. But rather than trying to impress, He tailored His comments to the person hearing Him speak. To a woman whose heart was parched, He spoke of quenching thirst.

How we speak to lost friends is directly related to knowing about their lives. Finding common ground about hobbies is not necessarily enough. We need to go deeper into the their lives and discover metaphors that connect with their need. For this anonymous Samaritan, the well represented everything that made her an outcast to the community. She came out in the middle of the day when it was hottest, most likely to avoid the other women in the community. Jesus' words about worship prompted her to express her interest in religious matters. Once He identified Himself as the Messiah, He brought out the evangelist in her. And it all began with the request for a drink of water.

People who feel guilty about their lives are often reticent to engage in religious conversations. Their guilt dissuades them from such lofty ideas as God, forgiveness, and freedom. As God's ambassador, you must access the common threads of life (water, breath, love) in order to engage those burdened with sin's guilt in conversations that lead to redemption.

Think of someone on your mission list who has a particular need. Identify a way you could make the connection from this need to the gospel.

Allow sin's full weight. One other issue we find difficult is allowing sin's full weight to fall on a person. Instead, we want everyone to feel good.

The Samaritan woman was guilty. She needed to be confronted by her sin so that repentance could follow. It is not God's intention to crush the human soul with unrelenting sorrow. But for redemption to take hold, we must first face our depravity. This woman's lust-filled life and philandering ways were the dominant forces in her life. Jesus could not allow her religious talk to overshadow the root of her distance from God—sin.

Dealing with sin is not pleasant. Our tendency is to comfort the lost and tell them that it will all be OK. But there is a time for us to confront sin and allow the Holy Spirit to do His work of conviction. All of us must face the hard taskmaster that is God's law and see how terribly we have failed to keep it. Then God will transform the thirst we thought we had for religion into a yearning to know the Messiah who brings life.

The Samaritan woman Jesus met was aware that the Messiah was coming and would explain everything (see v. 25). Prepare yourself for similar encounters. The guilt-ladened people around you are ready for redemption.
†

How might you begin to help a lost friend fully face the sin that has separated him from the Heavenly Father?

> Sometimes the best way for us to aid others burdened with sin's guilt is to remember the great weight that has been lifted from our own souls. Take time to read the following verses and identify what God has done to our sins: Psalm 103:12; Hosea 14:4; Micah 7:19.

DAY 3
Satisfied People

Good Teacher, what must I do to inherit eternal life?
MARK 10:17

Wealth is a relative term. For some people, wealth is a multilevel home in a gated community. For others, it is driving a sports car. But its status is something most people long to achieve. We push ourselves to the brink to find satisfaction through material possessions. Yet few achieve it.

Christ's encounter with the rich man in Mark 10 gives us insight into talking with people who are satisfied with their lives.

Set the standard. As the man approached Jesus, he had only one question: "Good Teacher, what must I do to inherit eternal life?" (v. 17). Mark even tells us that the man fell on his knees before Jesus to ask the question. It was a straightforward question by a powerful man who had unusually humbled himself.

The man facing Christ had a position of authority, many possessions, and a clean record. His life set the standard for success in his day. Jesus responded to his question by setting the standard of *who* is good instead of *what* is good. Though the man correctly identified Jesus as good, Christ pressed the man's gaze heavenward toward the Father. " 'Why do you call Me good?' Jesus asked him. 'No one is good but One—God' " (v. 18).

What questions do you think wealthy people ask themselves that would indicate spiritual hunger?

We often face similar circumstances in missional living. Every day we encounter successful, yet unsatisfied people. Having amassed possessions that do not spiritually satisfy, they look for more to do to gain righteousness. They may ask themselves questions like, *Why do I feel that something is missing? What should I do to make God happy with me? How can I go to heaven?*

Jesus' initial response was to draw out the man's allegiance to the moral law given in the Old Testament. Since childhood the man had kept all of the laws Jesus recited. So far he felt that he was on the path of earning the proper merit to receive eternal life.

Even in our day people come to the conclusion that their material possessions will not equal eternal life, but perhaps their works can. So they go on morality quests to appease God's judgment.

What kinds of actions do lost people take in an effort to earn righteous standing with God?

Be honest about the required sacrifice. I do not know what the man was expecting to hear from Christ. Perhaps he thought Jesus would pat him on the back and say, "Well done. Keep up the good work. You're in." His kneeling certainly suggested that he was willing to receive whatever instruction Jesus had for him. But Jesus' statement of what was needed in his life must have shocked this self-satisfied man.

What did Jesus ask the man to sacrifice?

Why do you think the man could not accept Jesus' conditions?

Christ defined our task when we encounter the materially and morally satisfied: we must show that even though they have achieved and obeyed excessively well, they still lack the one thing they need. We have few greater tasks than this—to ask satisfied people to give up their satisfaction. But to clearly communicate the need for the death of self so that the life of Christ can take up residence in our lives, there is no substitute.

Review your mission list (p. 158). Identify some things they would need to sacrifice to accept Christ.

▓ Self-reliance ▓ Complacency ▓ Pleasure ▓ Immorality
▓ Selfishness ▓ Pride ▓ Control ▓ Other:

Assure them of a better reward. The man's reaction was utter despair: "He was stunned at this demand, and he went away grieving, because he had many possessions" (v. 22). If only he had stayed at Jesus' feet to hear what He said next. The disciples, shocked by the exchange, asked how this "camel" could pass through "the eye of a needle" (v. 25). Jesus offered the hope needed by every person, including the satisfied ones: only with God's work is such sacrifice possible.

When we engage people who are satisfied with their earthly existence, our primary task is to show them the greatness of God's power. The young man left prematurely without hearing that the impossible task of giving away all is completely possible when empowered by the Almighty. Beyond that, the very reward he hoped to gain—eternal life—would be found in that sacrifice rather than in building his spiritual résumé on earth. †

> To lead others to abandon self, missional believers must do it first. Self-reliance is a great enemy in a believer's life. Spend time in prayer, asking the Spirit to show you where self-reliance exists in your life and how you can more deeply trust in God's power, such as a lack of contentment about possessions and physical appearance. Ask God to lead you to rely fully on Him so that you can more clearly display the power of the gospel.

DAY 4
Busy People

While they were traveling, He entered a village, and a woman named Martha welcomed Him into her home. She had a sister named Mary, who also sat at the Lord's feet and was listening to what He said. But Martha was distracted by her many tasks, and she came up and asked, "Lord, don't You care that my sister has left me to serve alone? So tell her to give me a hand." The Lord answered her, "Martha, Martha, you are worried and upset about many things, but one thing is necessary. Mary has made the right choice, and it will not be taken away from her.

LUKE 10:38-42

I loathe personality tests. Without fail I find myself characterized in a way I don't like. You may have the same reaction. The results might reveal that you are too antisocial, uptight, detail-oriented, or disorganized. Nevertheless, personality traits play a part in spiritual journeys.

When Jesus visited Martha's home in Luke 10, an all-too-familiar story unfolded, and it had much to do with the dispositions of the two main characters. Reread today's focal passage.

Two women. Two very different perspectives on Jesus' visit. Mary sat to listen. Martha scurried to prepare.

Which are you? ■ **Mary** ■ **Martha**

How does your personality color your relationship with God?

Have you ever tried witnessing to a Martha? They are so busy running about taking care of the details of life that there seems to be no time to sit and talk about any substantive idea. One of the first issues in ministering to a Martha is getting a time commitment. Their endless list of chores, hobbies, shuttling children, and late nights at work makes them a bit insufferable. But missional Christians must become experts in patience. Eventually, your Martha will pause just long enough to see that someone else (Mary) is actually sitting at the feet of the Master. And they will long for the same.

Who are some Marthas on your mission list? What activities seem to consume their time and energy?

With busy people you will need to provide plenty of opportunities for them to interact with you and other Christians. Once you have some time with them, it is critical that you make the most of it. Jesus went to the heart of the matter when Martha complained about her busyness. We should use the same quick wit and offer the same benefit. When Martha complained of her sister Mary's reluctance to work, Jesus pointed out that Mary had made a better choice and that what she gained would not be taken away. His lesson was to show Martha that conversely, she had chosen unwisely and what she had would not last.

The Marthas in our lives act the same way. They choose to be busy, complain about being busy, and then cry foul about those who are not busy. As we enjoy our lives walking in peace with Christ, we should offer them the way of escape because ultimately, their busyness is nothing more than a form of pride: "Look at how much more I can do—more than any of you." But this path will lead to the same destination as the Martha of Jesus' day: desperation due to distraction.

Identify any Marthas you know who seem to be desperate.

Like Christ, we must help Martha see that lesser things, not better things, distract her. Leading the conversation is critical to being an ambassador. Because distraction is a problem, you will need to get out in front of the conversation. Otherwise, Martha will dominate its course with her list of accomplishments done and to be done. Be quick and thoughtful to do two things:

1. Show interest in them as people, not producers.
2. Explain how your faith plays a crucial role in managing your life.

How does your Christian faith help you manage your life?

Marthas gain their worth from their productivity. Your mission in their lives is to show that your worth comes directly from the God who created and redeemed you, not from yourself. Use Scriptures that teach that Christ has completed all the work necessary for salvation. †

Pray for the Marthas on your mission list (p. 158). Identify ways you can help them slow down and see the life of Christ in both you and your church.

How could you or your family help a family of Marthas in your neighborhood?

- Provide dinner once a week at your home.
- Host a game night.
- Begin a spiritual-discussion group.
- Go out for coffee and dessert.
- Other:

DAY 5
Doubting People

"If You can do anything, have compassion on us and help us." Then Jesus said to him, "If You can? Everything is possible to the one who believes."

MARK 9:22-23

I find each of the four Gospels fascinating, in part due to its unique perspective. Mark is the most condensed of the four, not just for its length but also in the way it presents the encounters with Christ. Each is to the point.

One such account involves a desperate father. In Mark 9:14-29 Peter, James, and John have just come down from the top of Mount Hermon, where they saw Jesus transfigured along with the appearance of Moses and Elijah. After having witnessed one of the greatest moments in history, they would watch Jesus deal with doubt.

Approaching the crowd, they met several people:

- The (presumably) young man who had been possessed by an unclean spirit since his childhood
- A desperate family
- The other nine apostles, feeling dejected because they had been unable to drive out the demon
- Arrogant religious teachers
- The crowd looking to witness a magic trick

But let's turn our attention directly to one particular man—the father. He made two key statements that are relevant to our missional efforts to reach others with the gospel. When asked by Christ how long his son had been plagued by the evil spirit, he replied, "From childhood. … And many times it has thrown him into fire or water to destroy him. But if You can do anything, have compassion on us and help us" (vv. 21-22).

Jesus, being fully God, was not surprised by the man's statement but showed the perfect level of displeasure to make His point: "If You can? Everything is possible to the one who believes" (v. 23). Jesus had to address the conditional *if* in the father's statement. The man could just as easily have said, "But You can do anything" or "Since You can do anything." However, his disbelief had such a hold on him that he had doubts about the very One he sought to deliver his son from evil.

Examine your mission list (p. 158). Identify any who doubt the truth of who Jesus is.

How have you responded when they have expressed their doubts to you?

Our culture accepts doubt much too easily. In fact, doubt is often encouraged as a way to work through the process of faith. Some parents set their children loose to find their own religion or to abandon it all together. But we must stand alongside Jesus and counter any thought that *if* can be associated with the power of Christ!

As we present Christ to those outside the faith, we should not be shocked when they express doubt. But we must be ready to give the case for faith. Again, because Jesus has all knowledge, the father's *if* did not surprise him. Likewise, you and I should be saddened by doubt but not surprised by it. In fact, when doubt is finally admitted, the case for faith can be made. The father's second statement opened that very door: "Immediately the father of the boy cried out, 'I do believe! Help my unbelief' " (v. 24).

In an age of increasing spirituality, people want to believe in something or someone. But seldom will they express their struggle with faith. Missional living on our part should create the expectancy in others that faith is worthwhile. Our lives should engage them at their point of crisis in a way that creates a desire to have faith grow within them. Our proclamation of the gospel should stir their souls to the same cry of this desperate father: "God, help me believe as I should!"

Missional living never gives ground on the truth but always adjusts its communication method to best help those who hear the truth to understand it. After Jesus dealt with this father, He turned his attention to the nine apostles who had failed to cast out the evil spirit and taught them a profound lesson: "This kind can come out by nothing but prayer" (v. 29). Even with all their experience walking with Jesus and watching Him work, they still needed prayer.

Prayer is a tool in God's hand to guide us toward the truth revealed in Scripture and to press us in the right direction in life. When we become filled with pride, we no longer pray. Why? Because we believe in the power of ourselves. But when we are properly desperate for God's work in and through us, we pray. And then we pray well. †

Go before the Lord and ask Him to show you whether faith marks everything you do. What is there about you that would encourage faith in others or discourage a life of faith?

Doubt is a huge part of our religious culture. List Bible stories that have given you strength when you felt doubt creeping into your life. How can these stories encourage you to boldly witness and show compassionate ministry to the lost?

SESSION

5

Missional Spirituality

GROUP EXPERIENCE

SESSION GOAL

You will identify ways your private
devotional life with Christ
will shape missional living.

Missional Checkup

→ Describe how you began to classify your lost friends this week
in the categories of religious, guilty, satisfied, busy, and doubting.

→ Guilt and doubt can cause you to hesitate in missional ministry.
How did the stories you studied this week encourage you to
press forward as a missionary ambassador for God?

Spiritual Disciplines

→ What hindrances do you face in having consistent times
of prayer and Bible study?

→ Watch DVD session 5 and answer these questions.

What is the central discipline of the Christian life?

What impact do believers' devotional lives have on
missional living?

→ Read Psalm 119:64:

LORD, *the earth is filled with Your faithful love;*
teach me Your statutes.

→ When you hear the phrase *spiritual disciplines*, what type of
person comes to mind—a superspiritual person or an average
believer? Why do you have that reaction?

→ **List practices you would consider spiritual disciplines and describe the impact each should have on your walk with Christ.**

To this point our study has focused on how love motivates our work in God's mission.

→ **How might love be the compelling force in our devotional lives?**

→ **Read 1 Timothy 4:7-8:**

Have nothing to do with irreverent and silly myths. Rather, train yourself in godliness, for, the training of the body has a limited benefit, but godliness is beneficial in every way, since it holds promise for the present life and also for the life to come.

Many people spend a great deal of time dieting and exercising.

→ **Compare the effects of spiritual training with those of physical training, according to 1 Timothy 4:7-8.**

Though many practices can help us develop spiritually, the two most basic are Bible study and prayer.

Bible Study

→ **Read Joshua 1:7-8:**

Above all, be strong and very courageous to carefully observe the whole instruction My servant Moses commanded you. Do not turn from it to the right or the left, so that you will have success wherever you go. This book of instruction must not depart from your mouth; you are to recite it day and night, so that you may carefully observe everything written in it. For then you will prosper and succeed in whatever you do.

After Moses' death, God gave Joshua the task of leading the Hebrew people into the promised land. God's words in Joshua 1:7-8 address the place of His Word in Joshua's life.

→ **How does your private study of God's Word change the way you live on a daily basis?**

In order to live missionally, we have to understand God's mission as outlined in His Word.

→ **Do you have a process for examining and understanding a passage of Scripture? Discuss the way you read, understand, and apply a Bible passage to your life.**

→ When you study Scripture, how does having a missional perspective change the way you apply God's truth to your life?

Prayer

Another basic discipline of the Christian life is prayer.

→ What are common methods people use to pray more effectively? Consider methods like using a prayer list or outline or praying through specific components of prayer, such as ACTS—adoration, confession, thanksgiving, and supplication.

→ Jesus taught us how to pray in Luke 11:1-4. Discuss how each phrase can help you discover God's work around you and live missionally.

Father,
Your name be honored as holy.
Your kingdom come.
Give us each day our daily bread.
And forgive us our sins,
for we ourselves also forgive everyone in debt to us.
And do not bring us into temptation.

First Thessalonians 5:17 teaches us to "pray constantly."

→ How does constant prayer help us keep a missional perspective?

⟶ **Take two minutes to write down as many issues and people you could pray for in any given day.**

Additional Christian disciplines include fasting, Scripture memorization, meditation, spiritual retreats, submission, accountability, service, and fellowship.

⟶ **Discuss how God can use these and other disciplines to lead you on mission with him.**

Conclusion

Last week we learned that we need to contextualize the gospel message for our current place of ministry.

⟶ **How might our quest for a deep relationship with Christ relate to the culture we currently live in?**

⟶ **Close with prayer. Before the next group expereince, read the daily devotions for week 5.**

WEEK 5

Missional Spirituality

WHAT ARE SPIRITUAL DISCIPLINES?

The idea of discipline evokes either memories of angry parents or a reminder of why we have not lost that extra 15 pounds of weight. Yet having discipline in the spiritual realm greatly benefits believers. Paul wrote in 1 Timothy 4:8, "The training of the body has a limited benefit, but godliness is beneficial in every way, since it holds promise for the present life and also for the life to come." Being in the midst of God's work to fulfill His mission on earth requires great discipline.

The idea of spiritual disciplines has existed for centuries. However, many Christians have relegated such practices to pastors, monks, and superspiritual people. In contrast, all believers should perceive such spiritual activity as an expression of love for Christ. In fact, love is the central discipline of the Christian life. The common and uncommon practices called spiritual disciplines are tools that help us draw closer to God and show our love for Him.

What spiritual disciplines do you practice? Check all that apply.

- **Bible study**
- **Scripture meditation**
- **Scripture memorization**
- **Prayer**
- **Other:**
- **Worship**
- **Fasting**
- **Service**
- **Sacrifice**

How do these disciplines help you draw closer to God and show your love for Him?

The disciplines can be categorized as interior and exterior. Interior disciplines include Bible study, prayer, listening, watching, and silence. Such practices encourage us to be quiet before God so that He can direct our every thought and step. In showing our love for God in these ways, we grow in faith and obedience to God. The Holy Spirit teaches us truths from God's Word and helps us recall Christ's words in prayer. In our busy world, listening prayer, watchful minds, and periods of silence are welcome habits for those who seek God's wisdom to drown out the world's dissonance.

Exterior disciplines change the way we act. They include fasting, service, study, and simple living. Though we are not called to reject all physical possessions, the exterior disciplines help us prioritize spiritual nourishment over physical hoarding. Service and study are relatively familiar to us. Fasting and simple living seem to be contrary to our culture. Yet we are learning that missional living is often contrary to all of the world's cultures. Denying ourselves food in order to pray and meditate on God's Word seems to be a practice reserved for biblical characters. Yet this physical act is a wonderfully rewarding way to place our whole hope in God. Simplicity of life is much the same. God can teach us much about His priorities when we choose to live on less and trust Him for more.

Let God use spiritual disciplines to drive you deeper in faith and farther out on mission. †

How can your practice of spiritual disciplines affect your efforts to live missionally?

DAY 1
Study the Scriptures

As for you, continue in what you have learned and firmly believed, knowing those from whom you learned, and that from childhood you have known the sacred Scriptures, which are able to instruct you for salvation through faith in Christ Jesus.

All Scripture is inspired by God and is profitable for teaching, for rebuking, for correcting, for training in righteousness, so that the man of God may be complete, equipped for every good work.

2 TIMOTHY 3:14-17

The two central practices of the Christian life are Bible study and prayer. If you dedicate time to these two expressions of love toward God, you will find it easier to know His heart and will for missional living.

In the Scripture above, Paul encouraged Timothy to delve deeper into God's Word, which contains the mysteries God has revealed to humankind. But Scripture is not just a philosophical tome; it leads us to work out our faith in practical ways, which we could never dream up without God's help.

How are we to truly understand God's Word? We begin by holding a proper view of authority. When we study Scripture, God is addressing us; we are not dissecting Him. Our view of the Bible reveals the way we view God Himself. If the Bible is just one religious book among many, God is only an afterthought to us. But if we regard Scripture as God-breathed, we properly understand our place beneath God's sovereignty. Before us is the Word of God, which can "instruct you for salvation through faith in Christ Jesus" (2 Tim. 3:15).

Identify a time when God spoke to you through a specific Scripture. Based on that experience, how would you describe to an unbeliever the difference between Scripture and other literary works?

Believers must show a twofold devotion to the Scriptures. Ezra 7:10 says, "Ezra had determined in his heart to study the law of the LORD, obey it, and teach its statutes and ordinances in Israel." These two issues, study and observance, are reflected in the following principles for studying the Bible.

Bible study should be comprehensive. I strongly suggest that you read the entire Bible. The Bible on my desk is 1,094 pages. Reading such a long book seems a daunting task; but by reading three pages a day, you can finish it in a year. By reading 12 or 13 pages a day, you can read it in three months. There is simply no substitute for understanding the panorama of God's redemptive history.

Bible study should be consistent. By looking at your calendar and bank statement, I can tell what you truly value in life. If you logged the study of God's Word into your calendar, where would it rank? That ranking would reveal your commitment to God and His agenda. As needed, begin to remove less important commitments so that you can devote proper attention to God's Word.

Bible study should lead to clarity. Nehemiah 8:7-8 states that the Levites "explained the law to the people as they stood in their places. They read the book of the law of God, translating and giving the meaning so that the people could understand what was read." As the law was read to Israel, a great revival broke forth. The Levites had the task of bringing clarity to the Scriptures as they were read. Too often we read a passage and move on even if we did not understand it. Pause and make sure you have clearly understood how God is revealing His character and agenda in each passage.

Here are some questions you can ask about each Scripture text:
- What is the context?

- What is the genre—the type of literature?
- What was message to the original hearer?
- In what ways is God the hero and the main character?
- How is redemption explained?

Bible study should lead to obedience. Once we have learned to study the Bible more effectively, it should naturally lead not only to knowledge but also to a life that is obedient to Scripture. Our understanding never outpaces our obedience. Deuteronomy 29:29 reminds us, "The hidden things belong to the LORD our God, but the revealed things belong to us and our children forever, so that we may follow all the words of this law." The word *that* in this verse is crucial. The mysteries God reveals about His character and His ways are the impetus for our conformity to His character and His ways.

Bible study should engender devotion. Our obedience to God's Word should be an affectionate response. Though we should not be driven by emotion, it has its place. Are we not to love God with our heart as well as our mind, soul, and strength? When the law was taught in Nehemiah 8, the people wept as they listened to it (see v. 9). In your study of Scripture this week, do not forget to be in amazed; humbled; joyful; and, when appropriate, sorrowful in the truths you learn. †

Check the characteristics that are true of your Bible study.
- Is comprehensive
- Is consistent
- Leads to clarity
- Leads to obedience
- Engenders devotion

Circle a quality you would like to begin working on.

Studying Scripture directly relates to missional living. Review your mission list (p. 158) and note any Scriptures you need to share with specific persons.

DAY 2
Learn to Pray

*Sanctify them by the truth; Your word is truth. As You sent Me into
the world, I also have sent them into the world. I sanctify Myself
for them, so they also may be sanctified by the truth.*

JOHN 17:17-19

Home phone, work phone, cell phone, e-mail, IM, Facebook, text messages,
conference calls, video conferencing, VOiP, fax, and even snail mail—we
have no shortage of methods to communicate with one another. But what
about our communication with God? That's what prayer is all about.

Learning how to pray requires recognizing authority. Praying well begins
with knowing who began the conversation—and it was not we. Prayer is
our response to God's relational initiatives. All the authority in our prayer
belongs to God.

When you pray, what is your primary purpose?
⬛ **To ask God for what you need** ⬛ **To seek God's heart**

How does your answer affect the way you approach being on mission?

Ultimately, prayer is a conversation in which we express our love for God
by listening to Him and humbly making requests to Him. Prayer is a tool
through which God aligns our passions with His mind and will. It is a
place where He develops our faith, patience, and understanding of king-

dom work. In other words, prayer shapes our hearts to the form of God's missional endeavor.

Pray about God's work in the world. To pray well, we need to know what God is doing so that we can speak to Him about it and pray about our role in it. That's why we learned about Bible study yesterday. Because the Scriptures are God's inerrant revelation, we can fully trust them to show us His purposes and ways. We can also understand God's work by watching for His activity in our community and the world. We can discern God's work around us by answering questions about the people around us.

Ask God to show you how He is working in the lives of persons on your mission list (p. 158).

• **Who is open to conversing about spiritual matters?**

• **Who is suffering and needs to be comforted?**

• **Who has erected barriers about discussing the gospel?**

Take time to stop and pray for any persons you have listed.

As we become sensitive to the Holy Spirit's activity around us, then we will be able to pray with insight about our role in God's mission.

Carefully emulate the prayers of Jesus. In Jesus' prayer in John 17 we witness His deep desire for the glory of God to be known, for believers' sanctification, and for the unity of the church. To follow Jesus' example when we pray, we must first honor God and pray that the nations will yield to His glory. Recognizing that Christ spent such effort to pray about the

Father's glory should call us to do the same. To pray missionally, we should seek God's wisdom in declaring God's glory.

In what ways do you see your prayer life bringing glory to God?

Christ's call for Christians to be sanctified is a blessing to missional living: "Sanctify them by the truth; Your word is truth. As You sent Me into the world, I also have sent them into the world. I sanctify Myself for them, so they also may be sanctified by the truth" (John 17:17-19). Sanctification is the process by which God makes us holy in our moral character and choices. We should pray for God to make our character like Christ's. When our character comes in line with our Lord, our passion will follow His as well. Without being made holy by God, we would have no hope of receiving Christ's mission, much less participating in it. It is significant that within the context of Christ's plea for our holiness, He couched our commission to the world: "As You sent Me into the world, I also have sent them into the world" (v. 18). Prayer renews our minds and hearts, placing us in a position to follow God out of our place of prayer and into the mission field.

Define *sanctification* in your own words.

Why is holiness essential for missional living?

Pray about your holiness. Confess your sins and yield to God's sanctifying work in your life.

In John 17 Jesus also prayed for the unity of believers: "I have given them the glory You have given Me. May they be one as We are one. I am in them and You are in Me. May they be made completely one, so the world may know You have sent Me and have loved them as You have loved Me" (vv. 22-23). The unity in the church is to imitate the unity in the Godhead. Though an eternal mystery, the Bible reveals the love, humility, and singular purpose that exist in the members of the Trinity. Mirroring the Trinity, members of the body of Christ are to live as distinct individuals who are interdependent and who care for one another. †

Circle the number beside each characteristic to indicate how your church functions as the body of Christ.

	Poor			Effective	
Love	1	2	3	4	5
Humility	1	2	3	4	5
Singular purpose	1	2	3	4	5
Interdependence	1	2	3	4	5
Care for one another	1	2	3	4	5

The unity for which Christ prayed is more than harmony in a local congregation. Verse 23 shows us that our complete unity is part of missional living; it lets the world know that God has loved us and has sent us out! Once again, the issue for which we pray should affect the way we live God's mission.

Pray for unity of heart and purpose in your congregation.

DAY 3
Silence Before God

Guard your step when you go to the house of God. Better to draw near in obedience than to offer the sacrifice as fools do, for they are ignorant and do wrong. Do not be hasty to speak, and do not be impulsive to make a speech before God. God is in heaven and you are on earth, so let your words be few. For dreams result from much work and a fool's voice from many words. When you make a vow to God, don't delay fulfilling it, because He does not delight in fools. Fulfill what you vow. Better that you do not vow than that you vow and not fulfill it. Do not let your mouth bring guilt on you, and do not say in the presence of the messenger that it was a mistake. Why should God be angry with your words and destroy the work of your hands? For many dreams bring futility, also many words. So, fear God.

ECCLESIASTES 5:1-7

A parent must have coined the phrase "Silence is golden." Our lives are filled with talk, music, debates, and noise from every angle. In fact, we are surprised when there is quiet. Perhaps the volume of our lives is why we stutter-step in following God.

The Book of Ecclesiastes records Solomon's quest to understand the ways of God and find meaning in life. The passage above offers an odd respite to the meaningless searching.

In past generations silence was a virtue. In silence spiritual people would carefully consider God's Word and work in the world. Today we rarely find it and seldom seek it. But Solomon encouraged silence when we are before the Lord.

Notice the "bookends" of the passage. The first verse teaches a prudent walk before God. We should be circumspect and behave ourselves in the face of deity. Rather than making suggestions to God, we should "not be hasty to speak" (v. 2). The passage ends with what some call a warning and others term a gift: "Fear God." The fear of God should pervade our lives—not a terrifying horror but a stunned reverence resulting in endless adoration.

Review the passage and name some ways we are not to approach God.

How would these errors discourage a proper fear of God?

Solomon identified different ways people act before God when they pray.

- Verses 1-3 warn of speaking too much and commend humble silence.
- Verse 1 refers to a life that attempts to bribe God with foolish sacrifices. We are arrogant and impious when we think we can bargain with God. He is never impressed with our sacrifices but instead desires a clean heart that is ready to obey.
- Verse 3 describes a self-centered life born of vain dreams. Do you find yourself so busy that the only refuge is in daydreaming and fantasizing? Danger lurks in allowing our inner churnings to overrule God's speech.

- Verses 4-6 warn of a life filled with empty vows. Making a promise to God for fidelity and allegiance is not to be done hastily. If you foolishly make a promise and delay in keeping it, God will hold you accountable. There is nothing wrong with making great commitments to God, but don't make rash ones you cannot or will not keep.

Check any of the practices of which you are guilty when you pray.
Speaking too much in prayer
Vain dreams
Bargaining with God
Empty vows

In contrast to these vain practices, we should seek the God-ordered life shown in verses 2 and 7. Our prayers should be filled with the silent space that allows God to speak and direct our lives.

During my seminary days my theology professor strode into class with purpose one day and said, "Today I'm going to tell you the most important lesson you will learn in all of my theological lectures." We hastily took up our pens and prepared to write down the words of our esteemed professor. Then he said, "There is only one God, and you are not He." At first we chuckled and were a bit disappointed, but then the wisdom he had spoken and the implications for our lives settled into our hearts. "God is in heaven and you are on earth, so let your words be few. Fear God" (vv. 2,7).

To live missional lives, we must listen to the One who set the agenda. Let's be honest: you and your church have come up with some great plans for ministries that have failed miserably. Why? It could be because we told God about our plans for His church and never listened to His plan. We asked God to bless our vision for the future of ministry and never got His perspective on our future. We had a grocery list of needs for Him to care for and never listened to what He desired for us to do. †

Spend time in prayer. Repent of vain patterns of prayer that seek to advance your agenda instead of God's. Take time to be silent and stand in awe of God.

Now pray specifically about the life of your church and its role in God's mission. Jesus said the gates of hell would not prevail against His church. That means nothing can stop His agenda. So if your church is not prevailing, perhaps it needs to listen more closely to what God is saying. Today pray for your pastor and ask the Lord to bless him with a heart that clearly hears. Pray for the Spirit to teach your Bible study leaders the deep mysteries of Scripture so that they will be prepared to teach others. Pray that you will personally understand what role God has for you in your local congregation.

DAY 4
Feasting in the Fast

Whenever you fast, don't be sad-faced like the hypocrites. For they make their faces unattractive so their fasting is obvious to people. I assure you: They've got their reward! But when you fast, put oil on your head, and wash your face, so that you don't show your fasting to people but to your Father who is in secret. And your Father who sees in secret will reward you.

MATTHEW 6:16-18

Food is necessary. Without it you will die. However, food has become a social necessity as well. We eat to celebrate birthdays, holidays, promotions, straight A's in school, and everything else. Mealtimes are used to fend off both death and loneliness. They are occasions when we sustain life and build relationships.

For believers, however, there is a time to walk away from food. Jesus taught His followers to fast. Perhaps the operative word in the passage above is *when*. Jesus did not say "if" but "when." Christ assumed that believers would fast. He fasted, and He is the best example of a man on mission with the Father.

What is fasting? It is a spiritual exercise that alters your diet by eliminating food and/or drink in order to spend mealtimes in prayer. Simply put, you pray instead of eat. And prayer, as we have learned, is essential to missional living. Missional living is choosing the total subordination of our preferences to God's will. Fasting is a wonderful discipline through which we express our love for God and hear from Him.

Have you ever fasted? If so, how did it affect your walk with God?

How can fasting draw you closer to God's heart for others?

When we fast, we must ensure that we are doing it for the purposes of God's glory and mission. The purpose of fasting is not to earn extra points with God. God directed the Old Testament prophet Zechariah to ask the people, "When you fasted and lamented in the fifth and in the seventh months for these 70 years, did you really fast for Me?" (Zech. 7:5). And Jesus warned that we are to fast in the secrecy of our relationship with God and not for the praise of people. Fasting should be a physical sign of our utter need for God and a spiritual exercise in which we submit to him.

Fasting reveals the control food and gluttony have over our lives. In it we learn how childish our physical desires can truly be.

What foods do you depend on to lift your mood or to give you energy?

When I fast, I always realize how dependent I am on caffeine from my coffee to begin my day and how sugar in my tea keeps me in a good humor. Choosing to remove these substances from my day to give myself over to prayer and Scripture allows me to test exactly what controls my disposition. When I find that earthly substances hold such sway, I look for ways to further submit to the Creator's reign. It takes a belly truly scoured empty by hunger to learn that we do not live by bread alone but by God's precious Word (see Deut. 8:3).

Biblical examples of fasting reveal a variety of purposes for this practice.

- Public calamity (see 2 Sam. 1)
- Confessing sin (see 2 Sam. 12; Neh. 9)
- Facing temptation (see Luke 4)
- In worship and ministry (see Acts 13)
- Appointing leaders (see Acts 14)

In all of these examples God was meeting with His people or sending an ambassador. Missional living is consumed with both: speaking with God and speaking for God in the world. †

Consider the biblical examples of fasting we examined today. Check any circumstances you are facing.

- ▢ Public calamity
- ▢ Confessing sin
- ▢ Facing temptation
- ▢ In worship and ministry
- ▢ Appointing leaders
- ▢ Other:

Will you consider taking a fast to better hear from God?
▢ Yes ▢ No

DAY 5
Service and Humility

He must become increase, but I must decrease.
JOHN 3:30

In the 16ᵗʰ century Nicolaus Copernicus published the book *De revolutionibus orbium coelestium (On the Revolutions of the Celestial Spheres)*. In it he formulated the scientific basis for a view of the cosmos in which the earth is not the center. His proposition was controversial and heretical, but it was true. The earth is not the center of the universe.

To live missionally, we need a Copernican revolution of the soul. We must live with the realization that the world does not revolve around us. Our lives revolve around that which gives life to the universe—not just a third-rate star in the cosmos but the very Giver of life. And He has called us to His mission. As revealed in the life of Jesus, God's mission entailed Christ's humility before the Father and His service to humanity.

How did Jesus demonstrate humility before the Father?

How did Jesus demonstrate service to humanity?

The oldest sin of humanity is pride. Eve was tempted to eat the forbidden fruit and thus to become more than she was—to become like God. And people have chased that fruit ever since. Christians must learn to acknowledge our smallness before God. As we seek His glory and live in His mission, our own ego will naturally fall away. "He must increase, but I must decrease" (John 3:30) expresses the heart of a missional Christian.

Can you honestly say that you seek to decrease and allow Christ to increase as you live your life?

What attitudes and behaviors do you need to put to death in order to let Christ increase in your life?

Humility is an odd quality for human beings to value. To get ahead in this world, you must sell yourself, promote yourself, and look out for yourself. But in the Christian life we are to die to self. Because we are ambassadors for Christ, our daily agenda must become subservient to God's mission for us. It is humbling to think that all of our plans for life must be trashed. They are not plan B; they are nothing. Only God's glory and work must have any bearing for us. And His plan is for us to serve.

What plans do you need to scrap in order to get on God's missional agenda?

Service to others should be a believer's normal tendency. In the beginning, staving off vanity, stubbornness, and favoritism will seem like a full-time endeavor. The original sin in which we are born drives our minds to consider self first and rid ourselves of any other responsibilities. Furthermore, our culture of narcissism encourages self-centered behavior. Sometimes even in celebrations of those who do good for the poor, there exists a self-aggrandizement of the human spirit. All such posing is an affront to the life of Jesus, who "emptied Himself by assuming the form of a slave, taking on the likeness of men" (Phil. 2:7).

At the heart of missional living is giving up our rights and preferences. To be a missionary to a community, we must live in the culture of the lost and must serve them in ways that will connect them to the gospel. †

Spend time in prayer. Repent of any pride and humble yourself before God. Express your desire to be a servant who is on mission to your world. Ask God to give you a heart of service toward Him and others.

Consider five ministries you can engage in to meet the needs of persons on your mission list (p. 158).
- The ministry of the mundane—changing tires, helping a colleague, offering to care for children, taking out the trash
- The ministry of interruption—finding ways you can leave behind your agenda and let someone else's take its place
- The ministry of the sidekick—embracing your weaknesses and working alongside someone else in his or her strength
- The ministry of holding your tongue—choosing to encourage others in their achievements instead of showing everyone how much you know
- The ministry of bearing—choosing to move beyond merely tolerating people to loving them, even the difficult ones (see Eph. 4:1-3)

Write at least one name from your mission list beside each ministry. Ask God to show you how and when He wants you to carry out one of these ministries.

SESSION 6

Missional Obedience

SESSION GOAL

You will discover how your love for Christ is expressed in obedience to His commands, and you will identify ways to express love to lost people through your actions.

Missional Checkup

→ Describe practical ways you increased your time in the Word and in prayer this week.

→ How do you feel that spiritual disciplines will increase your affection for Christ?

Love and Obedience

Love is an element of our lives that is displayed through both emotion and action.

→ **How do express love to your family? To friends? To church?**

→ **Watch DVD session 6.**

What is the relationship between loving God and obeying Him?

John has become known to us as the beloved apostle. He sat next to Christ as the Last Supper, and he wrote more about love than the other three Gospel writers combined. Yet through all of this, he continually highlighted the role of obedience in his letters to the early church.

In contrast, culture seems to be obsessed with personal rights. When rules are emphasized, people often cry foul.

⟶ **When rules are given, why do people consider them so oppressive? Is the reason something childish in us or something more philosophical?**

⟶ **Read 1 John 5:3-5:**

This is what love for God is: to keep His commands. Now His commands are not a burden, because whatever has been born of God conquers the world. This is the victory that has conquered the world: our faith. And who is the one who conquers the world but the one who believes that Jesus is the Son of God?

God shows His love to us by giving directions for our lives.

List a few of God's commands from Scripture and discuss how they enrich our lives rather than burden us.

⟶ **Read 1 John 3:1-3:**

Look at how great a love the Father has given us that we should be called God's children. And we are! The reason the world does not know us is that it didn't know Him. Dear friends, we are God's children now, and what we will be has not yet been revealed. We know that when He appears, we will be like Him because we will see Him as He is. And everyone who has this hope in Him purifies himself just as He is pure.

We are called to be imitators of God. These verses teach us that our salvation brings us purity.

⟶ **How can moral purity display God's mission of redemption?**

⟶ **Read John 14:15-17,21,23-26.**

If you love Me, you will keep My commands. And I will ask the Father, and He will give you another Counselor to be with you forever. He is the Spirit of truth. The world is unable to receive Him because it doesn't see Him or know Him. But you do know Him, because He remains with you and will be in you. The one who has My commands and keeps them is the one who loves Me. And the one who loves Me will be loved by My Father. I also will love him and will reveal Myself to him. ... If anyone loves Me, he will keep My word. My Father will love him, and We will come to him and make Our home with him. The one who doesn't love Me will not keep My words. The word that you hear is not Mine but is from the Father who sent Me. I have spoken these things to you while I remain with you. But the Counselor, the Holy Spirit—the Father will send Him in My name—will teach you all things and remind you of everything I have told you.

As Jesus spoke about His departure from the earth and the arrival of the Holy Spirit, he said in John 14:15, "If you love Me, you will keep My commands."

⟶ **How does the Spirit make it possible for us to obey?**

Our allegiance is revealed through whom and what we love.

$\longrightarrow$ **For Christians, what competes for our love that would replace God's mission in our lives?**

The church encourages believers to consistently study the Bible and put into practice what we learn.

$\longrightarrow$ **Discuss the effects if our knowledge of Scripture outpaces our obedience to God.**

Obedience is the measure of our love for God.

$\longrightarrow$ **List practical ways you could begin obeying better and thus see love growing in your life through missional living.**

That Your Joy May Be Complete

$\longrightarrow$ **Read John 15:9-11:**

As the Father has loved Me, I have also loved you. Remain in My love. If you keep My commands you will remain in My love, just as I have kept My Father's commands and remain in His love. I have spoken these things to you so that My joy may be in you and your joy may be complete.

Jesus set an example for us through His humility and submission to the Heavenly Father. He wants us to be obedient so that we will have His joy.

→ **Share personal stories about how you have felt the joy of Christ when joining Him in missional living.**

Conclusion

Sometimes the road to obedience must begin again with repentance over past disobedience.

→ **To move your life into a missional position, what are some character flaws and sins you need to let go?**

→ **Close with prayer. Before the next group experience, read the daily devotions for week 6.**

WEEK 6

Missional Obedience

IDENTIFYING A MISSIONAL DISCIPLE

When asked whether they have a loving church, the vast majority of believers will say yes. The real test, however, comes when people outside the congregation are asked that question, when new people visit, or when someone new joins the church. As Jesus taught at the Last Supper, believers' lives should exhibit one overarching identifier: "I give you a new command: Love one another. Just as I have loved you, you must also love one another. By this all people will know that you are My disciples, if you have love for one another" (John 13:34-35).

Christ's new command followed His humble act of service to the apostles by washing their feet and His prediction of Judas's betrayal. Additionally, it came just before His prediction of Peter's denial. Jesus knew the hearts of His apostles, just as He knows ours. Jesus gave commands when people were not naturally following their tenets. He knew Judas's traitorous nature and Peter's arrogance. He knew the other 10 apostles would flee into the night when He was arrested. Jesus commanded His closest followers to love one another with the same sacrificial love He had demonstrated.

As Jesus observes your life, do you think He finds it necessary to remind you to love others?

A missional life is defined by its emulation of Christ. We are not to love in the best way we have seen in the world. Our love is determined by the way Christ has loved us. His love initiates a relationship with the unloving and sinful, and His love is expressed in service. We make much of Jesus' washing the feet of the twelve—even to the point that some churches have traditionally held foot-washing services. But it is not the act that is primary; it is the humble service that identifies the depth of our love for others. Missional believers must express our love for our neighbors through service.

In what ways are you serving others?

Our love must also show in our communication of the truth. When we study the greater context of Jesus' life, it is clear that He expressed His love for us by telling the truth about Himself and humanity's need for redemption. As He served the apostles by washing their feet, He didn't stop when their feet were clean. He went on to teach the apostles about the role of the Holy Spirit, impending joy, and prayer. We must show our love both by doing acts of service and by telling the gospel.

In what ways are you telling the gospel?

With courage we must test our witness before our community. Love, in its biblical form, stands as the banner that must be waved over the church and its missional believers. †

DAY 1
Love's Presence

"If you love Me, you will keep My commands. And I will ask the Father, and He will give you another Counselor to be with you forever. He is the Spirit of truth. The world is unable to receive Him because it doesn't see Him or know Him. But you do know Him, because He remains with you and will be in you. I will not leave you as orphans; I am coming to you. In a little while the world will see Me no longer, but you will see Me. Because I live, you will live too. In that day you will know that I am in My Father, you are in Me, and I am in you. The one who has My commands and keeps them is the one who loves Me. And the one who loves Me will be loved by My Father. I also will love him and will reveal Myself to him." Judas (not Iscariot) said to Him, "Lord, how is it You're going to reveal Yourself to us and not to the world?" Jesus answered, "If anyone loves Me, he will keep My word. My Father will love him, and We will come to him and make Our home with him. The one who doesn't love Me will not keep My words. The word that you hear is not Mine but is from the Father who sent Me."

JOHN 14:15-24

Jesus allowed no way to evade His intention. Love will naturally be followed by obedience. But alas, rebellion is our natural tendency, even toward those we love. Prodigal children, fighting friends, fractured marriages, and contentious congregations seem more the norm than loving relationships do. And then there is our roguish spirit toward the Lord who brought redemption. We need to nurture the loving obedience that Christ called for.

What struggles do you have in obeying Christ's commands?

What do you think is causing you to disobey? Check all that apply.
- A lack of love for Christ
- Preoccupation with the world
- Busyness
- Failure to yield to Christ's lordship
- Other:

Love is to be the enduring quality of missional living. Just consider how love played a role in our redemption. It is because of love that the Father sent the Son. It is by His love that the Son obeyed. It is in love that the Son died for sinful humankind. And it is in love that the Spirit came to indwell the lives of believers when the Son ascended to His throne room. God's offer of love to us is expansive in every way. Because we are to imitate God, love should color our entire manner of living.

In life we often follow the directives of people we do not love. Soldiers in battle follow their generals' commands because they want to win (and live). Employees do what their bosses dictate because they wish to be paid. Students complete their teachers' assignments because they want to pass their courses.

Our relationship with Christ is to be utterly different. We obey because we love, not because we are duty-bound or fear His reprisals. Christ-followers must strip the negative connotations from the word *obey*. People hear it and immediately think of oppressive leadership. Instead, believers should hear the ring of loving fellowship. Love's practical expression is in obedience. It only makes sense to follow the One to whom we have sworn allegiance.

But obedience is difficult for us. So how can we do it? The beauty of Christ's requirement for us to both love and obey is His knowledge that we can do neither very well on our own. So as He met with His disciples, He promised the presence of the Holy Spirit to help our infirmed souls. The Counselor's indwelling is an abiding presence of God's love and a teacher for our continued obedience. Missional living is possible only with God's empowerment. It is a mystery; we are called to be obedient. On our own we cannot. So God enables us so that His plan will be fulfilled. His love extends from the initial act of redemption all the way through our everyday obedience.

How does the Holy Spirit enable you to obey?

Christ's words come with a stern warning by which we should evaluate our lives. Verse 24 says, "The one who doesn't love Me will not keep My words." The question should be obvious: Do you obey? If the reply is no, then the conclusion is equally obvious: you do not love Jesus. No matter what you say, it is your actions that reveal your level of love for Christ. His warning should arrest our souls and demand an answer. †

Consider the past six months of your life. Were you disobedient to God in any missional opportunity? If so, take time to repent in prayer and seek God's direction to complete the work He has for you to do.

Now examine your mission list (p. 158) and think about the next six months. What are your missional opportunities to—
• witness to someone about the gospel?

• lead a new believer to a greater understanding of Scripture?

• help your church engage with your community?

DAY 2
Reviewing the Law of Christ

Brothers, if someone is caught in any wrongdoing, you who are spiritual should restore such a person with a gentle spirit, watching out for yourselves so you also won't be tempted. Carry one another's burdens; in this way you will fulfill the law of Christ. For if anyone considers himself to be something when he is nothing, he deceives himself. But each person should examine his own work, and then he will have a reason for boasting in himself alone, and not in respect to someone else. For each person will have to carry his own load.

GALATIANS 6:1-5

In week 1 we examined the law of Christ in Paul's teaching to the Galatians. Let's return to it to discover what it teaches us about missional obedience.

Sin is ugly. It is destructive. It results in death. To our credit, Christians usually try to avoid sin; but we often fail. And when we do, the help of friends is needed and appreciated.

As Paul taught the Galatians about their freedom in Christ, he was also led to write about what to do when someone falls into sin. I assume you are seeking to be spiritual in the sense Paul is writing about in verse 1. If that is the case, your goal is to fully imitate Christ. How did Christ teach us to confront others about their sin?

Fulfill Christ's law by joining God's mission of redemption. In the Gospels Jesus' work of calling the sinful to repent is constant. He confronted legalists, visited with sinners, and called a tax collector down from a tree branch so that He could go to his home. Jesus came "to seek and to save the lost" (Luke 19:10). Through this mission of redemption, Jesus showed deference to the Father in all things. The Gospel of John records that Jesus watched the Father to know what He should do next: "The Son is not able to do anything on His own, but only what He sees the Father doing. For whatever the Father does, the Son also does these things in the same way" (John 5:19).

You and I must follow Jesus' example in waiting on the Father. But notice Jesus' next statement in verse 20: "The Father loves the Son and shows Him everything He is doing, and He will show Him greater works than these so that you will be amazed. " Because of the Father's love for the Son, Jesus was not kept in the dark about His mission. Furthermore, this love would be extended to us and through us in the form of greater works.

Describe a time when the Father gave you directions about what to do, what to say, and where to go on mission with Him.

We live missionally because we want to be obedient to God's work of redemption in us. Our obedience to share Christ is a natural response to God's graciousness in allowing us to have a role in His great redemptive plan.

Fulfill Christ's law by bearing a burden you do not own. What does bearing another's burden look like? We are tempted to assuage other people's guilt rather than come alongside a truly broken life. We are quick to tell someone with a crumbling marriage, "Oh, it will be all right" and offer a spiritual platitude. Their reality is bleak, dark, and chaotic. Bearing their burden will take time. It will cost you dearly as you test the bounds of your friendship with them. With such a circumstance you will weep, laugh, grieve, and even confront these people you love. But isn't that what Christ did for us when we were far from His Kingdom? The same will be true when you—

- forgive someone's transgression against you;
- confront a friend caught in a web of alcoholism;
- counsel a friend whose parent has passed away;
- help a friend with a prodigal teenager;
- spend time with your pastor, who feels the weight of the world on his shoulders.

As you examine your mission list (p. 158), identify someone whose burden you need to bear. Describe the burden they are carrying.

What would be the cost of your helping to bear their burden?

Jesus bore the entire weight of God's wrath on our behalf. We can forgive a friend for a temper tantrum. We can show patience with lost neighbors who need us to walk with them toward the cross, even when it is a slow walk. Every time we bear a burden, we are blessed to share in the sufferings of Christ.

Confront and forgive. Missional living is about redemption, but it is first and foremost about truth. And Jesus is the truth (see John 14:6). He confronted people about their sin while offering forgiveness to those who repented. Be prepared to confront friends with truth of the gospel and to lead them to an encounter with the One who offers forgiveness. †

As you examine your mission list (p. 158), identify someone who needs to be confronted about their sin. Pray about any actions God wants you to take as you join God's work of redemption.

DAY 3
Completing Love

This is how we are sure that we have come to know Him: by keeping His commands. The one who says, "I have come to know Him," yet doesn't keep His commands, is a liar, and the truth is not in him. But whoever keeps His word, truly in him the love of God is perfected. This is how we know we are in Him: The one who says he remains in Him should walk just as He walked.

1 JOHN 2:3-6

Our efforts to love others often fall short. Even our word *love* does not always capture what we mean. We use the same word for loving God, loving our families, and loving pizza. To have a missional impact on others, we need to understand and practice Christlike love. How can we do that? It starts with knowing God.

We all want to know God. Why else would we invest time in Bible study, prayer, worship, and other means of spiritual growth? Because we love Him and wish to obey Him, thus knowing Him better.

In today's focal passage John issued a warning to those who claim they want to know God.

According to 1 John 2:3-6, what is the evidence that we know God?
■ Obedience   ■ Spiritual gifts   ■ Love

What is the result if we obey God's Word?

To say we know God means we obey Him. Otherwise, we are lying brag-garts. But a lying tongue cannot make up for a hypocritical life. It may cover it in front of others, but it will not fool God. In fact, He says we are devoid of truth if we claim to know Him while our lives are disobedient.

It should frighten us to think the truth would not pervade our lives as Christians. Scripture teaches that we should fear God with reverent awe. We should be terrified to live our lives outside His truth. Missional living is about the truth—both adherence to it and proclamation of it. And remember, Christ is the truth (see John 14:6).

John taught that if the truth lives in us, we will obey God's commands. And our obedience to God's Word will make His love complete in us. God's inerrant and sufficient Word is not merely for interesting reading or rule keeping. It is God's revelation of Himself to us. In it we discover His directives for knowing Him perfectly through Christ. And if we choose to follow it decisively, He can lead us on the journey of perfecting love.

As Christians, we lay claim to the life of Christ in us. We declare our dependence on Him and our independence from sin's stranglehold on our souls. As John said, it changes our lives: "The one who says he remains in Him should walk just as He walked" (1 John 2:6). And what did Jesus' life of love and obedience look like? It was unwavering, joyful, and holy. It focused on the glory of the Father and the redemption of humanity. Jesus came on a unique mission to provide a way of salvation for you and me. To walk as He walked, we must pursue the same path. The love Christ expressed gladly extended redemption. In offering that love, Christ did not play favorites. He met with Jew and Gentile, man and woman, child and adult, law keepers and rule breakers. And to all, He was willing to show God's love by proclaiming redemption through repentance and faith. †

Make room in your schedule for a time of repentance before God. Give the Holy Spirit utter freedom to expose the places in your life that are devoid of God's truth. Make a list of unheeded commands of God in your life—things you have violated or omitted. Repent and acknowledge God's sovereignty in your life. Express your love for Him and your desire to obey His commands. Ask for His help in obeying Him so that His love can be complete in you.

As you examine your mission list (p. 158), ask God to help you walk as Christ walked and to express His redemptive love to the unbelievers in your life.

DAY 4
Loving God's Word

Princes persecute me without cause,
but my heart fears only Your word.
I rejoice over Your promise
like one who finds vast treasure.
I hate and abhor falsehood,
but I love Your instruction.
I praise You seven times a day
for Your righteous judgments.
Abundant peace belongs to those
who love Your instruction;
nothing makes them stumble.
LORD, I hope for your salvation
and carry out Your commands.
I obey Your decrees
and love them greatly.
I obey Your precepts and decrees,
for all my ways are before You.

PSALM 119:161-168

As a parent, I sometimes find myself making a key error: expecting my children to obey a rule I have not taught them. Unintentionally, parents hope children will behave in a fashion we expect but have not clearly outlined. Although our children are smart, they aren't that smart! The only solution? Explain the code of conduct.

God has lovingly provided His revelation to us in the Scriptures. If we don't know the next step in obedience, we must search the Bible. In it we will learn about God's character and His plan for redeeming fallen humanity. A missional Christian, therefore, reveres and relies on God's Word for direction.

Psalm 119 is a celebratory song about the beauty of God's Word.

As you read the verses from Psalm 119 at the beginning of today's lesson, underline words that reveal the psalmist's attitude toward God's Word.

The power of the Word. The psalmist wrote, "My heart trembles at your word" (v. 161, NIV). What causes your heart to tremble? Is there a person or circumstance that literally causes you to shake and have sweaty palms? God's Word should hold such sway over believers' lives that we must obey it. We are not afraid, but we are captivated and moved by it.

The Word of God is different from every other piece of literature because it is divinely inspired. All other books are written from human intellect and imagination. In contrast, all the writing in Scripture is "inspired by God" (2 Tim. 3:16). Elsewhere it is described as a double-edged sword (see Heb. 4:12) and a light to our path (see Ps. 119:105).

In what ways does God's inspired Word have power?

How have you experienced that power in reading or applying God's Word?

God's Word has power because it displays God's wisdom and activity throughout history and in the world today. It gives insight into His character and our need for redemption. Furthermore, because the Holy Spirit lives in us, God's power is at work when we read Scripture, teaching us truth and helping us apply God's Word to our lives. The apostle Paul taught young Timothy that the Word of God is "profitable for teaching, for rebuking, for correcting, for training in righteousness, so that the man of God may be complete, equipped for every good work" (2 Tim. 3:16-17). To live missionally, we must teach, rebuke, correct, and train in righteousness. If left to our own devices to accomplish these tasks, we would degenerate into harsh masters demanding obedience to petty regulations. Obedience to God's Word releases us from the pressure to determine God's desires. We are simply to read and follow His instruction. And a missional Christian who obeys God's statutes finds that they reap abundant fruit in the Kingdom.

How does recognizing the power of God's Word change your attitude toward missional living?

Love for the Word. No other religious writings hold out the promise we find in the Bible. God speaks with authority through His Word. Only the Bible offers hope for knowing God personally through Jesus Christ. For that reason alone we should love the Word of God.

Psalm 119:162-165 speaks of the joy the psalmist holds because of God's revelation. He feels like a treasure hunter who has stumbled on a diamond mine. Like the ancient hymn writer, our hearts should also sing praises throughout the day for God's goodness as revealed in His Word. We should love the Word because it reveals God and brings peace. †

How would you explain to a lost person why you love God's Word?

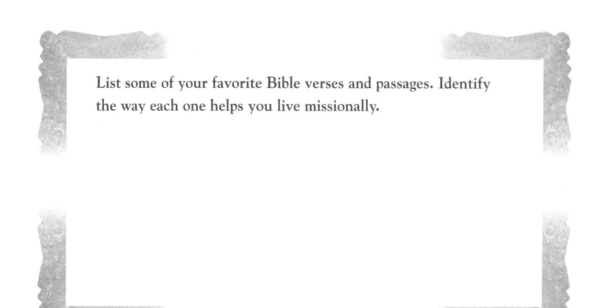

List some of your favorite Bible verses and passages. Identify the way each one helps you live missionally.

DAY 5
Love's Victory

This is what love for God is: to keep His commands. Now His commands are not a burden, because whatever has been born of God conquers the world. This is the victory that has conquered the world: our faith. And who is the one who conquers the world but the one who believes that Jesus is the Son of God?

1 JOHN 5:3-5

Our mortal understanding of obedience is one of subservience. The very word *obey* sounds like something we might yell at our dog. But as John explained, obedience in the realm of God's kingdom is associated with freedom.

Read 1 John 5:3-5 above. How would you explain to an unbeliever the freedom that comes with following Christ?

John was writing to a dispersed group of Christians to warn them about false teaching infiltrating the church. In explaining the need for pure doctrine, he also emphasized the need for a pure life. In fact, the two are directly related. When our knowledge of who God is and what He desires matches our obedience to His commands, we can experience joy.

We sometimes think of joy as the absence of a burden, for example, when we have finished a difficult project or have been relieved of a stressful problem. We should not mistake God's commands for such toilsome issues in our lives. Verse 3 reminds us "His commands are not a burden." It is in disobedience that we find the violent, heavy weight of the world. In obedience, however, we are liberated to participate in the victory God has already won (see John 16:33). Consider your obedience to answer His call to salvation. When you placed your faith in Christ, He allowed you to inherit victory over sin due to His work on the cross. Victory also comes in every moment of the Christian life when we bow before the King.

Obedience will bring victory over the temptations we face daily. Personal sin will obviously take us far from missional living. It will interrupt our ability to discern the work of the Spirit and to participate in His compelling work in others' lives. Our dedication to missional living comes with a commitment to habitual holiness.

Missional Christians want others to experience the victory we have received by our faith in Christ. Furthermore, Jesus instructed us in His Great Commission to teach new believers to "observe everything" He has commanded (Matt. 28:20). Missional ministry includes delivering the gospel, but it does not end there. Our missional perspective must include the desire to lead others in the victory that comes through everyday obedience.

Describe a time when you experienced the joy of Christ when you joined Him in missional living.

John asked, "Who is the one who conquers the world?" (1 John 5:5). Who can triumph over all creation? That's a daunting task—but completely possible! John identified those who can achieve this victory: "the one who believes that Jesus is the Son of God" (v. 5).

Consider this verse's ramifications for missional ministry. As people of faith, we already have victory over the world! Culture, sin, death, and judgment have no grip on our lives. We are free to live God's mission without fear of failure, because God assures victory throughout His kingdom. We can confidently move forward on mission with God, knowing that His will cannot be thwarted. It will be accomplished. †

Describe your missional activity during the past six weeks of this study.

What will victory look like in that missional ministry?

The Son of God has overcome the world. Where does your heart most burn for Him to work in your life?

Pray diligently for God to shape your heart to imitate the missionary nature of Christ's life so that you will purposefully bear witness to His redemptive love.

SESSION

7

Launching into Mission

SESSION GOAL

You will identify some things
you have learned during this study,
and you will set some goals for
missional living in the future.

Missional Checkup

→ **What did you discover to be God's current missional assignment for you?**

→ **How did you verbally share the gospel this week?**

→ **Describe a significant change you are making in your life to more fully reflect the redemptive mission of Christ.**

Review

Over the past six weeks we have evaluated our motivations for living God's mission.

⟶ **How is God's heart the standard for missional living?**

⟶ **How is Jesus' life on earth the example for missional living?**

⟶ **How have your ideas about love changed during this study?**

⟶ **Discuss some of the primary lessons you have learned over the past six weeks about the role of service to others in missional living.**

⟶ **Watch DVD session 7 and answer these questions.**

Why is missional living the most joyful thing we can do?

What supernatural resources are available to us when we abandon ourselves to God's mission?

Toward Missional Living

→ **Read Ephesians 3:14-21:**

For this reason I kneel before the Father from whom every family in heaven and on earth is named. I pray that He may grant you, according to the riches of His glory, to be strengthened with power in the inner man through His Spirit, and that the Messiah may dwell in your hearts through faith. I pray that you, being rooted and firmly established in love, may be able to comprehend with all the saints what is the length and width, height and depth of God's love, and to know the Messiah's love that surpasses knowledge, so you may be filled with all the fullness of God. Now to Him who is able to do above and beyond all that we ask or think according to the power that works in us—to Him be glory in the church and in Christ Jesus to all generations, forever and ever. Amen.

→ **Paul prayed that the church would be "rooted and firmly established in love" (v. 17). How will having love as your foundation change the way you engage your neighbors on behalf of the gospel?**

Sometimes when we look into our community, it feels impossible to reach them with the gospel. But Paul highlighted that God can do "above and beyond all that we ask or think" (v. 20).

→ **What are the "above and beyond" things you hope to see God do through you and your church?**

Ed Stetzer spoke about three principles from Philippians 2 that Christ exhibited:

1. He did not consider Himself (see v. 6).
2. He emptied Himself (see v. 7).
3. He humbled Himself (see v. 8).

Believers should have the same humble nature of Christ.

→ **In what ways has humility been difficult in your life when you were trying to be on mission with God?**

→ **How can you change the way you act toward unbelievers?**

→ **Discuss how our private devotional lives and missional living are linked. Specifically discuss how your private devotional life is helping to launch you into God's mission.**

The hope of Paul's prayer in Ephesians 3 is that believers will be filled with the "fullness of God" (v. 19). The missional perspective of Christian living calls for God's glory to be lifted above all other issues.

→ **How can your life more clearly begin to reflect God's glory?**

→ **How could your group continue to help one another remain accountable in being missional in lifestyle and perspective?**

Conclusion

The point of missional living is to see God honored through the redemption of people.

→ **Whom does God want you to reach by being on mission with Him?**

→ **End this session by praying for those to whom God is sending you.**

My Mission List